What Is To Be Done?

What Is To Be Done?

A Dialogue on Communism, Capitalism,
and the Future of Democracy

Alain Badiou and
Marcel Gauchet

Moderated by Martin Duru and Martin Legros

Translated by Susan Spitzer

polity

First published in French as Alain Badiou and Marcel Gauchet, *Que faire? Dialogue sur le communisme, le capitalisme et l'avenir de la démocratie* (c) Philo éditions, Paris, 2014

This English edition (c) Polity Press, 2016

Polity Press
65 Bridge Street
Cambridge CB2 1UR, UK

Polity Press
350 Main Street
Malden, MA 02148, USA

ISBN-13: 978-1-5095-0170-0
ISBN-13: 978-1-5095-0171-7 (pb)

A catalogue record for this book is available from the British Library.

Library of Congress Cataloging-in-Publication Data

Badiou, Alain.
  [Que faire? English]
  What is to be done? : a dialogue on communism, capitalism, and the future of democracy / Alain Badiou, Marcel Gauchet.
    pages cm
  Includes bibliographical references and index.
  ISBN 978-0-7456-0170-0 (hardback : alk. paper) -- ISBN 978-0-7456-0171-7 (pbk.: alk. paper) 1. Communism. 2. Badiou, Alain--Interviews. 3. Gauchet, Marcel--Interviews. 4. Democracy. 5. Capitalism. 6. Political science--Philosophy. I. Gauchet, Marcel. II. Title.
  HX73.B6314 2015
  335.43--dc23
                              2015019876

Typeset in 11 on 14 pt Sabon by Servis Filmsetting Ltd, Stockport, Cheshire
Printed and bound in the UK by CPI Group (UK) Ltd, Croydon, CR0 4YY

The publisher has used its best endeavours to ensure that the URLs for external websites referred to in this book are correct and active at the time of going to press. However, the publisher has no responsibility for the websites and can make no guarantee that a site will remain live or that the content is or will remain appropriate.

Every effort has been made to trace all copyright holders, but if any have been inadvertently overlooked the publisher will be pleased to include any necessary credits in any subsequent reprint or edition.

For further information on Polity, visit our website:
politybooks.com

Contents

Foreword
The future of an alternative
Martin Duru and Martin Legros

[W]e are not children to be fed on the thin gruel of "economic" politics alone; we want to know everything that others know, we want to learn the details of *all* aspects of political life and to take part *actively* in every single political event. In order that we may do this, the intellectuals must talk to us less of what we already know and tell us more about what we do not yet know and what we can never learn from our factory and "economic" experience, namely, political knowledge. You intellectuals can acquire this knowledge, and it is your *duty* to bring it to us in a hundred- and a thousand-fold greater measure than you have done up to now; and you must bring it to us, not only in the form of discussions, pamphlets, and articles (which very often – pardon our frankness – are rather dull), but precisely in the form of vivid *exposures* of what our government and our governing classes are doing at this very moment in all spheres of life. Devote more zeal to carrying out this duty.

This appeal to the intellectuals to take responsibility for freeing their fellow citizens from the domination of "economic politics" and for enlightening them, through "vivid exposures," about what it is possible to change in all spheres of life dates from ... 1902. It was written by Vladimir Ilyich Ulyanov (a.k.a. Lenin), in a pamphlet entitled *What Is to Be Done?*,[1] a work that left a lasting mark on history since, a number of years before the 1917 revolution and the Bolsheviks' seizure of power, Lenin theorized in it the idea of the vanguard revolutionary party.

More than a century later, this appeal has acquired new relevance and resonance. Aren't we once again, even if in very different ways, prisoners of a politics that reduces everything to economics? Don't we feel the need for a political knowledge of things, which would enable us to take part in a different, and better, way in the events of our times, instead of submitting to them as a destiny? And don't we hope that the intellectuals will abandon the abstract arguments of their "pamphlets and articles" and challenge the direction in which the governments of the day are taking our history? In 1902, at the time those lines were written, the future was an open question. The democratic and industrial revolution begun in the eighteenth and nineteenth centuries was only just starting to take hold in France and England, while Germany and Russia, roiling with turmoil, were still imperial regimes. Liberals, conservatives, and socialists competed for the European people's votes, while the communist movement was gradually developing by asserting its independence from social democracy. This was moreover one of Lenin's key

---

[1] V. I. Lenin, "What Is to Be Done?" in *Collected Works*, vol. 5, tr. Joe Fineberg and George Hanna (Moscow: Progress Publishers, 1960).

questions in *What Is to Be Done?* To counter the power of capitalism, which approach should be opted for: reform or revolution? Should the workers' movement be left to organize itself on its own or should revolutionary ferment be introduced into it from outside, through a party with a genuine political project? In any case, no one at the time suspected that the continent would be engulfed in two world wars, an unprecedented financial crisis, and the growing power of fascist, Nazi, and communist totalitarianisms . . .

So, oddly enough, here we are, a little more than a century later, after the short, tragic twentieth century, back at the same questions as Lenin's. Of course, the Berlin Wall did fall. For a short time, liberal democracy and capitalism even appeared to have won out for good, thereby fueling the over-hasty theory of an "end of history." But now an acute sense of a radical crisis of democracy and capitalism has returned, raising the question of their long-term survival. Even if the totalitarian systems have lost all legitimacy, Lenin's perplexity in the face of the future's uncertainty in 1902 has become ours again. Even the hypothesis of communism, which had seemed to be completely dead, rendered invalid by the fiasco of its historical realization, is regaining currency in the intellectual sphere and within the protest movements that are springing up all over the world. Reform or revolution? Capitalism, socialism, or even communism? It's as if the wheel of history had begun to spin again: *rien ne va plus*, all bets are off, we have no idea where we are going. Hasn't liberal democracy been shaken to its very core by the impact of capitalism, and isn't capitalism undermined from within by the power of finance? Hasn't politics lost all capacity to guide history? Does the communist hypothesis, stripped of its totalitarian trappings, offer a credible solution? Or can democracy reinvent itself to meet the challenges of globalization?

To tackle these issues head-on, we sought out two major figures of the contemporary philosophical scene: Alain Badiou, the leader of the current movement for a return to the communist idea, and Marcel Gauchet, the thinker of liberal democracy. Even though they seemed destined to cross each other's path and exchange ideas, they had oddly enough never met before. No one, up to now, had suggested the idea of a substantive dialogue to them – which goes to show that real opponents face off too rarely on today's intellectual scene. And that real debates are scarce, too often avoided.

Alain Badiou no longer needs any introduction. Born in Morocco in 1937 to a traditionally socialist family, a graduate of the École Normale Supérieure, influenced by Sartre, Althusser, and Lacan, among others, he was indelibly marked by the events of May '68 and the Cultural Revolution in China – which led him to head up a Maoist group, the Marxist-Leninist Union of Communists of France (UCF-ML). As a professor at Vincennes and later at the École Normale Supérieure, where he now teaches a seminar, he developed a demanding philosophical system, set out in his two major works, *Being and Event* and *Logics of Worlds* (both published by Éditions du Seuil, in 1988 and 2006 respectively, and in English translation by Continuum in 2005 and 2009 respectively). Breaking with some of his contemporaries who proclaim the end of metaphysics, Alain Badiou has sought to re-establish the discourse on being – what is traditionally called "ontology" – on the basis of mathematics, and set theory in particular. He has also proposed a new way of connecting the concepts of event, subject, and truth. A subject, for him, is someone who is faithful to a foundational event, which brings about a truth capable of orienting life (a truth of a political, scientific, artistic, or amorous nature). Apart from his academic works, which are studied all over the world and have helped, particularly in France, to revive interest in metaphysics, he has in the past 15 years or so become known to a wider public through polemical essays on contemporary politics, such as his short book *The Meaning of Sarkozy* (Lignes, 2007; English translation, Verso, 2008), which met with a resounding success. Generally speaking, in connection with his longstanding Maoist heritage, he stresses the need to revive "the communist hypothesis," the only one, in his view, that can offer a real alternative to the "parliamentary capitalism" to which democracy has been reduced. Along with other figures on the far left, such as Antonio Negri, Jacques Rancière, and Slavoj Žižek, he has participated in many conferences on the concept of "communism," which have met with an enthusiastic response among young people.

Marcel Gauchet's itinerary was very different. Born into a working-class milieu in 1946 in Poilley (Lower Normandy), and a graduate of the École Normale des Instituteurs [a prestige college for elementary school teacher training] in Saint-Lô, this self-educated man resumed his studies in the heady atmosphere of May '68, when he was introduced to political thought under the auspices of two pillars of the "Socialism or Barbarism" group, Cornelius Castoriadis and Claude Lefort. In little journals such as *Textures* or *Libre* he dedicated himself to the rediscovery of the political [*le politique*] and of democracy, in opposition to the hegemony of Marxism and the denial of totalitarian oppression, which prevailed at the time among the French intelligentsia. After a first book co-written with Gladys Swain, *La Pratique de l'esprit humain* [The Practice of the Human Spirit] (Gallimard, 1980, new edition 2007), in which he took apart the theories put forward by Michel Foucault in his *The History of Madness in the Classical Age*, he published a highly controversial book in 1985 (English translation, Princeton University Press, 1999), *The Disenchantment of the World: A Political History of Religion*, which viewed Christianity as the "religion of the exit from religion." Since then, he has been attempting to think Western modernity as the advent of autonomy on both the individual level, with the rise of human rights, and the collective level, with the emergence of the political form of the democratic nation-state. After becoming editor-in-chief of the journal *Le Débat* and director of studies at EHESS [Écoles des Hautes Études en Sciences Sociales] in the Centre de recherches politiques Raymond-Aron, he began a major undertaking, *L'Avènement de la démocratie* [The Advent of Democracy] (three volumes of which have already been published by Gallimard). At the same time, he paid constant attention to the new pathologies of contemporary democracy, in particular in *La Démocratie contre elle-même* [Democracy Against Itself] (Gallimard, 2002). With the warning he issued in 1980 – *Les Droits de l'homme ne sont pas une politique* [Human Rights Are Not a Politics] – he was one of the first to show that the threats hanging over the democracies are no longer outside, in external enemies seeking to destroy them, but within themselves, in the perversion of their own principles. Democracy, in his view, has become incapable of governing itself as a result of sanctifying its citizens' independence at the expense of the sense of the collective.

Badiou versus Gauchet. There was something intriguing about the match right from the start. People aghast at Badiou's constant, glowing references to the Cultural Revolution and Maoism and skeptical about or frankly hostile to the very idea of a revival of the communist idea could look forward eagerly to seeing him pitted against one of the most preeminent theoreticians and proponents of democracy. Conversely, people who are of the opinion that thinkers of anti-totalitarianism like Marcel Gauchet have paved the way for a re-legitimation of the neoliberalism that is partly to blame for the current crisis could also rub their hands in glee at the thought of seeing him debate one of the most consistent and harsh critics of contemporary liberalism. As both these public figures also have a reputation for being real fighters, capable of battling it out with their ideological opponents without flinching, the "fight" promised to be exciting. It didn't disappoint, even if, as you'll see, it took us completely by surprise.

Originally, the two thinkers were supposed to meet only once, in the context of *Philosophie Magazine*'s special edition, entitled "Philosophers and Communism," which came out in March 2014. The intensity of the first encounter prompted us to propose that they continue the *disputatio*, and they both immediately agreed. In the end, they met on three separate occasions, for almost three hours each time, and in three successive places with highly symbolic significance: first, the headquarters of the French Communist Party on the Place du Colonel-Fabien in Paris, a futuristic building put up by the Brazilian architect Oscar Niemeyer between 1966 and 1971; second, the Lutetia, a luxury hotel where the actors of globalized capitalism now stay whenever they're in Paris; and finally the Éditions Gallimard, a Mecca of intellectualism, where, just for the record, one of Alain Badiou's manuscripts was once rejected . . .

What were we struck by during these three sessions? The atmosphere and the tone, for starters. There had been two pitfalls to fear. First, the avoidance of debate, where the two philosophers would just sit there glaring at each other, presenting their respective points of view mechanically without comparing and contrasting them. And, at the other extreme, the stifling of the debate by a spirit of polemics, with outrageous caricatures, insults, and ad hominem attacks into the bargain. The match had promised to be a tough, head-on one, and it was, in terms of its content, but, in terms of its form, it took place in an exemplary atmosphere of openness and courtesy, not without a certain cordiality even – there was a lot of hearty laughter – although, at the same time, the gulf between the two sparring partners was growing wider and wider.

Aside from the calm atmosphere, what also caught our attention was the shift in the center of gravity of the debate. We had thought the debate would revolve around the past, around the meaning of the communist experience in the twentieth century and whether it was essentially totalitarian or not. That crucial issue was naturally dealt with, rigorously and abundantly. Faced with Marcel Gauchet, for whom the respect of pluralism is one of the great lessons that must be learned from the totalitarian period, Alain Badiou had to acknowledge that he "[wasn't] sure whether the problem of enemies [could] be resolved in the democratic framework." Nevertheless, we gradually realized that their real disagreement wasn't about that. Why? Because as far as both of them are concerned, the issue of totalitarianism is no longer topical. In Marcel Gauchet's view, historical communism has collapsed for good, and the totalitarian business has folded. In Alain Badiou's view, Stalinism betrayed and perverted the communist idea by entrusting its realization to the state, and we now need to rediscover the original creative force of the idea. Neither of them thinks totalitarianism in the strong sense of the term will ever come back. The real dangers lie elsewhere. Where? Right here, in the once again gaping conflict between democracy and capitalism. Can democracy regain control over a financialized capitalism that imposes its logic and hegemony all over the world? That's the bet Gauchet, who hopes to put the economy back under collective control, is making. By "taking capitalism apart," deconstructing it from within, the political will be in a position to control capitalism's inner workings and its aberrations. Alain Badiou, on the contrary, thinks that that cause has already been lost, because capital, as his shock phrase has it, is the "big Other of democracy," and democracy is subjected to it in its very essence. That is where the beating heart of the discussion lies. It also involves two completely different diagnoses of the current world situation.

What kind of world are we living in in these early years of the twenty-first century? Alain Badiou thinks that, after the collapse of the socialist states, we are returning to the normal course of a capitalism driven by a global imperial logic. To which Marcel Gauchet responds that globalization cannot be reduced to the economic dimension alone. As he sees it, globalization brings with it the promise of a "de-imperialized," "polycentric" world, in which no power, however dominant it may be, can dictate its law any more. In short, the debate gave rise to totally different opinions across the board. And battle lines as clear as they were deep emerged: on the one side, a far-reaching reformist vision that calls for a resurgence of democracy to restrain globalized capitalism, and, on the other, the idea of a radical change that would break with both capitalism and representative democracy. The specter of Lenin is lurking . . . but the very terms of the fundamental choice (reform or revolution?) he set out have been reformulated.

So what is to be done? In their dispute, Alain Badiou and Marcel Gauchet lay out in detail the approaches they each recommend – readers will judge for themselves and perhaps decide between the alternatives offered them. Without judging anything in advance, let's conclude with one last surprising fact: after they had battled it out over all the issues, our two philosophers ultimately agreed, at the very end of their exchange, to make a deal. Yes, a grand alliance. What did it involve? We're going to prolong the suspense and just say that the two opponents were able to see that there might be an advantage for each of them in moving ahead together: that the democratic reformist might be in vital need of the communist hypothesis to have a chance to achieve his own ends, and vice versa. In this ultimate agreement, in which Rousseau took over from Lenin as the reference, there was the same desire to restore genuine meaning to politics as the only sphere in which a collective universal can emerge. To believe in politics again, to convince ourselves that we haven't finished with it: perhaps that, above all, is what we should and can do.

Chapter 1
The encounter with communism

To begin this dialogue, we'd like to propose that each of you say a few things about the importance of communism in your itinerary. This is the first time you are meeting. You come from different political and intellectual backgrounds. But communism has played a vital role for each of you. Before turning to the historical experience of communism and its philosophical definition, could you explain how you discovered it – the idea as well as the movement and the political regime?

Alain Badiou: I'm a latecomer to communism. I come from a social-democratic tradition originally. My father, Raymond Badiou, a member of the Resistance, was the Socialist mayor of Toulouse from 1944 to 1958. So it was quite natural that I should start out as a militant in the French Section of the Workers' International (SFIO), which was the equivalent of the French Socialist Party at the time. As a student at the École Normale Supérieure, which I entered in 1956, I started a socialist group along with my friend Emmanuel Terray, even though communists abounded there. But my real political birth certificate dates from the Algerian War. Back then, I was viscerally revolted by colonialism and the horrors that were taking place during the war – torture was going on everywhere, even in the Paris police stations. I got involved in the bitter struggle against the policy of Guy Mollet's Socialist government, which had taken a repressive line against the uprising. The heightened tension within the parliamentary left led to the breakup of the SFIO. My father, who was also committed to the fight against the Algerian War and had resigned as mayor of Toulouse as a result of his opposition to the official government line, eventually founded the Unified Socialist Party (PSU) along with some other people. I was actively engaged in these developments and was a militant in the PSU until the late 1960s, even serving as federal secretary for the Marne Department – with some success, moreover, since I quintupled the PSU's results in the legislative elections!

Marcel Gauchet: They should have held on to you . . .

A.B.: Yes, I had a great opportunity to rise into the upper ranks of the party hierarchy . . . Who knows what might have happened had it not been for May '68! It was a shock wave, a profound upheaval in my personal and political subjectivity. I was 31 at the time. That was when I broke away from parliamentary socialism and really converted to communism. However, this new militancy didn't lead to my joining the French Communist Party (PCF), which was very powerful at the time. I have never been a member of it or a fellow traveler. And for good reason: I'd already found the

PCF to be too cautious in the anti-colonial struggles. When it came to the new revolutionary experiments, in the late 1960s and beyond, the PCF was, if anything, the enemy. A despised and very real enemy: the "official" militants wanted to hold on to their political monopoly in the factories. They prevented my friends and me from reaching out to the workers on the shop floors and from distributing flyers in the suburban markets. There were frequent, often violent, altercations between us. No, the communism that I gradually became affiliated with was certainly not represented by that bureaucratized party, so heavily dependent on the regime in power in the USSR. My communism was embodied in one of the French versions of Maoism, with the key event being the Cultural Revolution – which I'll come back to later. At any rate, my trajectory ran counter to the dominant pattern: while many militants, whether intellectuals or not, started out as communists before repudiating that heritage and moving on to something else, I, for my part, was "born" a socialist and became a communist!

M.G.: My itinerary was the exact opposite ... I come from a rather modest social background: my father was a road worker and my mother a seamstress. I was brought up with Gaullism and the most traditional Catholicism, from which I would later have to forcefully break free. We lived in the Manche department [Lower Normandy], and out in the country: the traces of communism were non-existent, to say the least. We wondered what it could be like! My first encounter with communism was intellectual in nature: I was overwhelmed when I read Marx and Engels' *The Communist Manifesto* at age 15. It was a moment of sheer exhilaration. Marx is the most dazzling writer I've ever read. He is without a doubt the philosopher who has mattered most to me, in the most lasting way. Practically speaking, I discovered politics in the final years of the Algerian War. My initiation experience was the repression of the anti-war demonstration that resulted in a number of deaths at the Charonne metro station in Paris on February 8, 1962. The novice Marxist that I was became acquainted at that time with the PCF in the guise of its militants. I was dumbfounded by this encounter and immune ever after to the PCF. What arrogance, what a capacity for manipulation there were in the so-called "conscious vanguard of the Party!" It seemed as though they were moving their militants around like chess pieces, as though they were maneuvering them solely in the interests of the party apparatus. I might have encountered friendlier people, more open practices, more substantial intellectual content . . . But I didn't, and everything that happened thereafter only confirmed my original distrust. As you've no doubt gathered, I've never been either a member or even a sympathizer of the PCF. Instead, I was involved with another, unofficial version of communism: what was called at the time "councilism," a term that's quite difficult to define. The councilist movement is part of the anarcho-syndicalist tradition. It focuses on the participation of the masses in decision-making, on direct democracy, but always within the scope of the communist idea in the broad sense of the term. Back then, this councilist movement was very fragmented and split into little rival factions, sometimes with no more than a dozen people in them. It was an underground movement, a minority within a minority, something that's never easy and is often disheartening . . .

Then May '68 happened. At first I was in my element, because the event marked the triumphant entry of ultra-leftism, of which councilism was one of the forms, onto the intellectual scene. My militant decision seemed to have met with a resounding confirmation at that time. And yet, a turning point had been reached. This is when our respective paths diverged: where, for you, May '68 paved the way for commitment to the communist idea, for me the failure of the movement – hardly surprising as such – and especially its consequences led me to a gradual, heartbreaking abandonment of my original Marxism. Little by little, I realized that communism was a model that could only lead to a dead end and that Marxism's very premises plunge us into insurmountable problems. I came to think that real political work could only be done within the framework of democracy – not the naïve democracy of my youth but democracy *tout court*. I felt it was necessary and urgent to rethink, to thoroughly reform, that certainly flawed but still improvable framework. The new focus was on making representative democracy advance and move forward. I'd been "born" a Marxist and I became a (critical!) fellow traveler of the Socialist Party. So that's how I entered the channel of "bourgeois politics," as I used to say condescendingly when I was young!

What role did philosophy play in your respective political and militant trajectories? Who and what were the major figures and intellectual currents that influenced the positions you took?

A.B.: My first essential influence was Sartre. When I was involved in the anti-colonial movement at the time of the

Algerian War I was a convinced existentialist. I knew the great maxims by heart. My grounding in Sartre went far beyond anything the philosopher explicitly wrote about colonialism: I undertook a diligent, enthusiastic, and patient reading of *Being and Nothingness*. From the end of World War II on, Sartre himself embodied the idea that philosophy was intimately linked to politics. This was the famous figure of the politically engaged philosopher. This combination of creative intellectuality and political militancy is typically French, and Sartre rightly saw himself as an heir to Enlightenment thinkers such as Voltaire and Rousseau. His incomparable prestige stems from his inclusion in that tradition.

M.G.: Indeed, in France there's a belief that politics should be combined with intelligence. This is a feature very specific to our country. The US is in this respect a perfect counter-example. There, politics is pure pragmatism: the problem is winning elections . . . Apart from the case of Sartre, the extraordinary prestige of communism in the post-war period was undoubtedly linked to the connection you mentioned: the communist idea sought to bring together the theoretical and practical dimensions, to combine thinking and political activism. France was an ideal breeding ground, so to speak, for it. And it still seems to be so today . . .

A.B.: You're ratting me out! I'm French to the core . . .

M.G.: I'm sure you are!

A.B.: For me, the interrelationship between philosophical engagement and political engagement is the driving force. But I want to point out that its meaning is far from obvious. It's quite a complicated, open question, which I'm still grappling with today. In terms of my personal development, philosophy has obviously played an important role in my political subjectivity – with Sartre being the first milestone here – but my political subjectivity, in conjunction with real facts (the Algerian War, May '68, the Cultural Revolution, and so on), also had a strong impact on what I agreed to regard as "real" philosophy. For this reason, I had to deal with the Marxist tradition in much greater detail starting with my adherence to Maoism in the post-'68 years. Ultimately, I developed a critical analysis of that tradition at a relatively late date. But the main point is that my political engagement was like the backdrop to what I had set myself as my proper philosophical task. When you fight for emancipation, against the colonial or capitalist order, you quickly encounter what is called a "subject" in philosophy. It's impossible to take up the issue of political activism without proposing a reasonable and reasoned theory of the subject, since there's always a dimension of will in politics that can't be eliminated. Consequently, following on precisely from my "conversion" to the communist idea, I began to tinker around with the idea of the subject. This entailed effecting an improbable, risky synthesis between the Sartrian legacy – in which the subject is something Sartre calls the "for-itself," and the for-itself is pure freedom, or, in other words, pure nothingness – and structuralism.

Could you explain the issues and modalities involved in that synthesis by putting us back in the context of how it was developed?

A.B.: In the mid-1960s, structuralism, the generic banner under which writers, sometimes of very different stripes, gathered, posited that the way society, knowledge, history, language, and so on function is determined by objective fundamental structures, invisible and "unconscious" substructures. Structuralism brought a breath of scientificity to the intellectual scene, and I welcomed it to some extent – I'm also a mathematician by heritage (my father was a math teacher), by personal inclination (I enjoy overcoming the resistance of a difficult problem), and by training (I've taken courses and seminars on formal logic and pure mathematics). It was clear that one of the prime targets of the structuralist current was the classic concept of the subject or consciousness. The Structuralists deconstructed the idealist conception of the subject as the source of all meaning and experience – which was still the conception of the dominant phenomenology of Sartre and Merleau-Ponty. The notion of the subject was reduced in various ways to the status of an object for science, of a bogus or even bourgeois category. This seemed philosophically modern to me; I identified with that materialist slant. But, from another angle, I thought structuralism went too far, precisely as regards the issue of the subject. Strip it of certain idealist attributes, sure, but structuralism sought purely and simply to eliminate it, to take away all its relevance and legitimacy in the order of philosophical discourse! This was the case, for example, with Althusser, one of my masters and at the time the leader of the movement for a scientificized Marxism. For him, history was a subject-less process, an a-subjective determination. I've never been Althusserian when it comes to this issue. For me, there is a subject, and that notion must be retained, while also taking account of structuralism's advances. If the subject is definitively eliminated, political activism is no longer thinkable or tenable. In fact, I note that those whose adhesion to communism was based on a background of this sort couldn't stick with it and ended up throwing in the towel. The very short horizon of total scientificity, the exclusive recourse to rigid structures – all this ultimately undermines political engagement and dooms it to a dead end.

At the time, there was someone else attempting a similar synthesis: Lacan. That's the reason for my admiration for him and my ongoing debate with him. In his milieu of psychoanalysis, Lacan made the subject contingent on the transindividual structure of the unconscious, associated with language. In so doing, he was part of the structuralist movement. But he was nevertheless determined to preserve and even re-establish the notion of the subject on that basis. Of course, in his occupation as a clinician, sitting behind the couch, he encountered subjects every day, and what subjects they were, what a condition they were in! Lacan sometimes defined himself, with his customary sense of provocation, as "the Lenin of psychoanalysis" – with Marx being the equivalent of Freud in psychoanalysis. But he was actually completely uninterested in politics; he couldn't have cared less about it. Maoism? Temporary stupidity. And he was resistant, to say the least, to the May '68 movement. Clearly, he wasn't on our side. Therefore, you had to take inspiration from his philosophical gesture concerning the subject but model it in a different way so that a new conception of it could draw on the new political situations and allow for new militant forms in them. So these have been my sources of inspiration. As they're so different from one another, they have made me a somewhat unusual philosophical figure.

Marcel Gauchet, you mentioned how important Marx was to you . . .

M.G.: Yes, and my admiration for him only grew when I undertook an in-depth study of Hegel, the philosopher who made Marx's work possible in a way, who at any rate stimulated him profoundly. Hegel is out of fashion today, unfortunately.

Your close personal and intellectual relationships with certain great figures of anti-totalitarianism such as Cornelius Castoriadis and Claude Lefort are well known. But was structuralism also important to you?

M.G.: Of course! It was the landmark intellectual event of the 1960s, after all. The real breakthrough occurred in 1965 . . .

A.B.: And it reached its peak in 1966.

M.G.: Right, it all went so fast! It's remarkable, when you think about it. In the same year, Lacan published his *Écrits*, Foucault, *The Order of Things*, Althusser, *Reading Capital*, Benveniste, the first volume of his *Problems in General Linguistics* . . . There was so much that was new! French structuralism, which is essentially a structuralism of the human sciences, unstuck the thinking of the Sartrian heritage and more generally of phenomenology as a whole, while at the same time entering into a critical dialogue with it. As everyone knows,

Heidegger was very important to Lacan, Foucault, and Althusser. The convergence of all this research, at the intersection of anthropology, history, and metaphysics, heralded a unified science of man and society through the element of language. As for me, structuralism went hand in hand with and contributed to the distance I'd taken from my original Marxism. Where you and I are concerned, Alain Badiou, we were out of sync with each other, once again. Structuralism, with the figure of Lacan, led you to a theoretical rehabilitation that was useful for revitalizing the communist idea. It had the opposite effect on me: an about-face and an ultimate abandonment of Marxism. We prove the saying that all thinkers are children of their time, except that very different trails can be blazed through the same landscape ... Marxist-influenced structuralism was repellent to me. I thought Althusser, who intended to strip Marxism of its humanist trappings, was creating a mystification of Marx's thinking, to put it a bit harshly. He claimed he could separate out the scientific and ideological elements in Marx's work, in the name of a materialist science that had disturbing similarities to the dogmatism prevalent at the time in the Stalinist PCF ... His Marx was highly implausible, and his rehabilitation ultimately led to a skeletal catechism. Within the ultra-left, there was a much more correct and stimulating reading of Marx. The fact remains, however, that, thanks to structuralism, a question Marx had neglected suddenly came fully to light, the question of the relationship between the individual and the collective. Marxism was disappointing in one respect: it seemed to promise a subjective emancipation, but in the end it always comes back to the model of the strict, rigid determination of individuals by the economic structures of society or by the anonymous march of history. Althusser favored this analytic framework. But in the work of other structuralist thinkers – and this is why reading Lacan was a shock for me, too – the possibility of a real linkage between the two levels, subjective and "objective," was starting to emerge.

In what way? What general set of problems did structuralism lead you to?

M.G.: How can what happens in what is commonly called our "inner life" be connected with what occurs in collective life? How are "the inside" and "the outside," "private" and "public," bound together? The concept of "structure" – structures of the mind, including language, and social structures, including classes and the rules of exchange – was supposed to provide an answer to this question. But in reality the notion of structure fails to provide a real understanding of the way a subject relates to the community to which s/he belongs. At best it provides an objective formalization of that relationship. It doesn't allow it to be understood from within. Aside from linguistic, economic, and psychic structures, it's actually the political that holds the members of a society together. And it's in the sphere of the political that the individual constitutes him/herself as a social human subject. That's the insight I developed, following in the footsteps of thinkers like Claude Lefort and Cornelius Castoriadis, by approaching the issue of the political quite early on from the perspective of its historical transformations. The issue I would gradually turn to, in the wake of structuralism, was the reinter-

pretation of history in a non-Marxist way: history as
the very locus of the interpenetration of the individual
and the community, and history as a guideline for present action. To undertake something meaningful, you
have to know where you're coming from, what your
theoretical and practical perspectives are. On the basis
of knowledge of the factual and intellectual past, we can
determine a general orientation within which a will, to
use the strong word you used a moment ago, can operate. Without philosophical insight into the historical
situation facing us, political action can only be blind. I
have stuck with this matrix, which, although simplistic,
is very effective.

The reinterpretation of history I've devoted myself to
has unfolded in two main directions: a genealogy and
in-depth study of the democratic experience in Europe,
but also an inquiry into the deep meaning of the unique
experience of historical communism, essentially in the
USSR.

A.B.: Fine, let's turn to history then . . .

Chapter 2

From Marx to Lenin

First theorized by Marx, communism became embodied in history beginning in 1917 with the October
Revolution, in which the Bolsheviks seized power.
How do you assess the transition from the idea to the
concrete experience of communism in the USSR? In
particular, do you think the regime established by Lenin
corresponded economically, politically, and ideologically to Marx's original conception?

Marcel Gauchet: When the word "communism" is used,
an ambiguity needs to be cleared up. A careful distinction must be made between communism as an idea, a
philosophical and social project, and communism as
a historical experience, led by the regimes that called
themselves by that name. As far as the idea is concerned,
it existed before Marx, even if it was he who gave it its
philosophical prestige. He reinterpreted the communist
project within the framework of a science of history,
which took the form of a succession of modes of production: primitive, slave, feudal, capitalist, and so on.

The evolution of human societies was determined by the primacy and transformation of economic structures. In this way, Marx broke with any idealist conception of communism; with him, a materialist philosopher, the idea came down from the intellectual heavens to the material earth below. It was the end of "utopian socialism," in favor of "scientific socialism," to use his friend Engels' terms.

How can we break free from capitalism and establish communism? For Marx, the key is the abolition of private property and the collective appropriation of the means of production. The latter is supposed to eliminate the divisions within society: the antagonism between bourgeois and proletarians, between capital and labor, but also between the state and civil society, city and country, men and women. It is also a question of putting an end to the division between the very idea of society and its real movement. In short, Marx's communist project promises a sort of great reconciliation, the advent of a society free of its divisions, which are painful disorders linked to a primitive state of the system of production. In every sphere, the aim is a harmonious totality. As regards this desire for the One, it's clear that Marx's thinking, almost in spite of itself, lends itself to a possible totalitarian-type capture.

That's what would happen in the USSR after the Bolsheviks seized power. The historical development of the communist project can be summed up in one word: Leninism. The notion of Marxism-Leninism was forged, and Leninism was defined in the orthodoxy as "the Marxism of our time." But, in keeping with an early conclusion that I subsequently developed further, I consider Leninism to be a pure and simple betrayal of Marxism. Lenin betrayed Marx in every way. That doesn't mean that Marxism is necessarily true! It means that we shouldn't blame Marx for what Lenin was responsible for. And I'm amazed to see the extent to which most critics have gone along with the common idea that Lenin was a Marxist. No, Lenin was the very opposite of Marxism, albeit incorporated in Marxism itself. We're confronted with an extremely complex alchemy.

What is it?

M.G.: On the one hand, of course, there was a certain continuity with regard to the ideas. Lenin took whole swaths of Marx's theoretical arsenal, in particular the conception of the process leading to a communist revolution. But, on the other hand, as regards political practice, the gulf between them is enormous. Why? Marx thought that capitalism, doomed in his times to increasingly severe recurrent crises, was heading toward implosion. Furthermore, he thought that the working class would grow stronger, become aware of its situation, and make the transition to communism on its own. This would require a short period of dictatorship of the proletariat to support and consolidate the transition from revolutionary disorder – itself coming after capitalist disorder – to a real communist society. In short, with Marx, everything was foreordained and programmed, as it were. Conversely, and here's where the basic difference between them comes in, Lenin didn't think any determinism led to the revolution. In his view, the rupture wasn't "natural"; it needed to be forced. Rather than relying on it to occur spontaneously, the revolutionary process had to be methodically planned out.

Of course, the times and circumstances were very different in 1917 from what they had been in 1848! Marx couldn't count on widespread support. Scattered throughout Europe, "his" workers comprised a rather quixotic International in terms of its capacity for effective action. It's understandable that praxis wasn't his primary concern and that he didn't have any real political thinking – or a very clear view of what would happen after the revolutionary transition. Lenin, for his part, came on the scene at a time when the workers' movement was a lot stronger, including in Russia. Such a development posed urgent problems of organization and definition of immediate and long-term objectives. In view of this, the revolutionary rupture, according to him, needed to be coordinated and steered. It had to be entrusted to an appropriate body that would be designated as the vanguard revolutionary Party. If the Party wasn't established, if it was lacking, socialism would remain an idle dream; the proletariat would end up succumbing to the charms of social democracy and would turn away from the revolution – and capitalism would continue even amid the worst atrocities. This is the famous "socialism or barbarism" alternative, which was later thematized by Trotsky.

That was the basic philosophico-political shift: Lenin "invented" the conscious, organized revolutionary party, whose goal was to seize the state and then destroy it. Once the October Revolution was achieved, the Party presented itself as the organ of transition to communism and became the cornerstone of the regime. It was armed with a doctrine, Marxist science, which purported to be the embodiment of the science of history. This Marxist science was externalized from the historical movement and the proletariat and mastered only by the regime's experts and officials. The Party was thus "justified," not only in imposing its ideology on society as a whole but in advancing society to the scientific stage of its functioning! A real political and ideological dictatorship was implemented, and all collective life was regulated and controlled by the Party. I use the term communist "ideocracy" to denote this sort of political and intellectual monopoly, which means a totalitarianism in the strictest definition of the term.

After Lenin died in 1924, Stalin took this logic to its extreme. Stalinism was the exact continuation of Leninism and drew the full consequences of its premises – just as Lenin had overturned Marx, so too did Stalin remain a loyal Leninist. The only particularity of Stalinism was circumstantial in nature: Stalin's main problem was to expropriate the peasants and accelerate the industrialization of the USSR. That resulted in a sort of new civil war, between the Party and the peasantry. That situation led to the implementation of a terrible system of terror.

Alain Badiou, what's your reaction to this analysis?

Alain Badiou: I think certain points of disagreement are going to come up . . .

M.G.: Finally! The readers must be getting impatient!

A.B.: Your analysis of the transition from Marx to Lenin seems far too cut-and-dried to me. As regards the political history, the continuity was much more significant than you suggest. In reality, there was a thread connecting the two figures with regard to the central issue of insurrections. Ultimately, the nineteenth century in the broadest sense was that of great revolts, from the storming of the Bastille in 1789 to the Paris Commune in 1871, by way of the uprisings throughout Europe around 1848. You mentioned the lack of any strong political thinking in Marx. That's exactly right. This man, educated by his youth as a revolutionary militant, harbored a sort of spontaneism, an over-confidence in the general forces of history, which would bring forth his program naturally. Marx believed that pre-history (that of private appropriation, the development of capitalism and class struggle, etc.) would give rise to real history, which coincides with the advent of communism as a finally non-pathological form of the organization of human societies. The Marxian conception was based not only on a general eschatology – the famous "*Grand Soir*" ["Great Evening"]. It was part of a context that derived to some extent from the French Revolution, a context in which the model of historical ruptures was precisely the insurrectionary model. Thus, if Marx had no real political thinking it was because he believed deeply in insurrectionism, as he himself had taken part in it in Germany in the 1840s.

Yet, 30 years later the tragic failure of the Paris Commune occurred. Following a spectacular new revolt, workers occupied and governed a major capital city for almost two months, and it all ended in a blood-bath, with horrible repression. Marx himself was not in favor of the uprising in the conditions of the time, but the Commune and its failure posed new problems for him. The Commune marked both the high point and the stopping point of nineteenth-century insurrectionism. On its ruins a question arose that would come to haunt the political debate: should insurrection still be maintained as an effective, legitimate model for proletarian revolution? Some said no, in particular the social democrats, who were in the majority in France and Germany. They ended up renouncing the idea of revolution. They joined established parties, choosing the path of "parliamentary cretinism,"[2] a path you yourself chose, Marcel Gauchet. (*Laughter.*)

But others continued to believe in the viability of insurrection ... This is where Lenin, whom I'd essentially define as a thinker and activist of politics, comes in. Like Marx before him, he took stock of the Commune's failure. Like his illustrious predecessor, he singled out the leaders' – admittedly flagrant – irresponsibility and concluded that there had been a tragic lack of organization in the movement. On that basis, he formulated the hypothesis that an insurrection can still be victorious provided it is led by a specialized, militarized, and extremely disciplined apparatus. As he would later say, "Insurrection is an art," which means: politics is not the same thing as the science of economics and history; it is a separate thought-practice.

And in 1917 that gamble paid off, against all the odds! The history of Leninism is the history of the absolutely unlikely success of that hypothesis. Which

---

[2] "Parliamentary cretinism" is a term used by Marx in *The Eighteenth Brumaire of Louis Bonaparte* to deride the notion that socialism could be achieved by parliamentary means.

goes to show that you sometimes need to pay attention to hypotheses, however unlikely they may be ... What triumphed with the 1917 revolution was the Leninist conception of politics as an art of situations and opportunities, in which subjectivity and organization were the highest priorities. But Lenin would have forever remained a relatively obscure theorist and activist if his views on political practice hadn't been borne out on the ground. Circumstances, in this case, played a key role. For his conception of politics to work, it required the appalling slaughter of World War I, the unique situation of Russia, engaged as it was in a different type of development from that of the European powers, and so on. The fact remains that we entered "the period of victorious proletarian revolutions" – that, among other designations, was what Marxism-Leninism was called. I remember that I myself read and studied closely the *Manual of Insurrection* that was distributed and studied at the time of the Third International.

So were you inspired by it?

A.B.: Not really! I never succeeded in believing that I could trigger a victorious insurrection by myself. Let's go back to Russia and Lenin. Once power had been seized, it had to be used to achieve communism, which is a whole other story. The challenges that arose were unprecedented. How do you collectivize agriculture in actual practice? How do you go about centralizing industry, establishing new forms of trade? Nobody had a clue! The task of transforming society overall was essentially assigned to a state conceived of in the image of the militarized revolutionary party. What was initially only a tool of transition, a machine for seizing power by force, became the exclusive model and basis of real power. The Soviet regime was really a barracks socialism . . . They wound up with a "dictatorship of the proletariat" – because the Marxian notion was revived – that was constituted in an extremely aggressive, violent way. The habit acquired during the terrible, brutal Russian civil war, which consisted in resolving all problems by liquidating the "enemies" identified as responsible for these problems, was retained and became the norm. When you're in the midst of a civil war, that method isn't completely unjustified. But when it's a question of building a state, it has devastating, barbaric consequences: as soon as some decision doesn't produce the desired results, you launch a purge to defeat internal "enemies." It's easy to proudly announce that the traitors have been defeated, but the fact is, the real problems remain. The culture of violence permeated Bolshevism so deeply that it blinded it. When you get to that point, communism as Marx defined it is a million miles away . . . It is simply nowhere to be found.

The original communist idea was gradually deformed and degraded in the USSR in the twentieth century: that's my conclusion, too. But the overall interpretation of Leninism that I propose differs from the one Marcel Gauchet put forward. Seen from the perspective of its historical origins, it is a brilliant and victorious political invention, but it's also the last incarnation of nineteenth-century insurrectionism, in which Marx had placed all his hopes. If the "realization" of the communist project in the USSR ended up being completely abandoned in actual fact, it was because of unresolved political problems in the stage that came after the seizure of power, not because of the project per se.

M.G.: Your interpretation, albeit partly correct, seems totally inadequate to me. It fails to reveal the true meaning of the Leninist and, after it, the Stalinist experience. That the 1917 victory validated the nineteenth-century insurrectionist model, yes, of course, you're right. I have no major objections to that. But what happened in the USSR goes well beyond that one aspect. If historical communism only boiled down to what you say about it, if the issues were limited to the contingencies peculiar to Russia, the extraordinary prestige of the Bolshevik regime and its ideology would be incomprehensible. Its significance and exceptional hold over people's minds wouldn't be fully appreciated. You have a sort of deflated view of the Soviet experience, Alain Badiou, which fails to grasp its full significance.

A.B.: I'm not going to get into an argument here. Up to now, I've limited my analysis to the seizure of power and the sequence immediately thereafter, the Russia of 1922–3, in which revolutionary excitement was still pervasive. Even if, here and there, I've already expressed serious reservations and even definite misgivings, my aim was not to propose a complete and final explanation of the Soviet political construction.

M.G.: Yes, but that's just it! It's that explanation that's called for. We need to go beyond the opening sequence. We need to take a larger step back and look at the bigger picture. This would involve not considering the USSR in isolation. Historical communism can't be dealt with apart from what happened at the same time in Italy and Germany, that is, apart from a thinking of totalitarianism. To understand the Soviet experience, an in-depth study of totalitarianism itself has to be undertaken.

Chapter 3
Totalitarianism

Marcel Gauchet, why, in your view, is the concept of totalitarianism needed to think communism as it was realized in the USSR?

Marcel Gauchet: I think that without a comprehensive analysis of totalitarianism we'll remain in the dark about the USSR. Why? Because fascism and Nazism constitute a sort of monstrous double of communism. At first glance these regimes seem like opposites, but we need to think their essential relatedness.

Alain Badiou: I don't much like the term "totalitarian." The idea of totality strikes me as being sort of tacked on to this business. I think the barbaric experiences of certain countries in the twentieth century have more to do with disorder, war, powerlessness, and a headlong rush forward than with totality. Furthermore, you talk about relatedness, but we're dealing with two radically different state politics: the rhetoric and politics of the Nazi state have an identitarian substrate – the constitutive anti-Semitism of the Hitlerian madness – whereas the rhetoric of the Soviet state was internationalist in nature.

M.G.: Relatedness doesn't mean sameness. I'm not claiming Hitler and Stalin were the same. It's hard not to see the radical hostility there was between the two sides! For a communist, there was no worse enemy than a fascist, and vice versa. But where the totalitarian regimes were concerned, there was a structural homology in that very antagonism. They had something in common, a kinship behind the façade of glaring differences.

What is the matrix shared by fascist, Nazi, and communist regimes?

M.G.: Let's put the rise of totalitarianisms back in a wider historical context, which has to do with the experience of political modernity. I define modernity in terms of a centuries-long process, which I call "the exit from religion." I use that phrase to avoid the more simplistic and inadequate ones of "secularization" or "laicization." A major, complex transition took place: modernity gradually got us out of the mode of collective structuration that had hitherto dominated the whole human past, namely, the religious mode of structuration. This religious mode was a *heteronomous* mode of structuration insofar as it was defined by the subjection of human societies in all their aspects (organization of power, relationships between people, economic and social forms, and so on) to the law of the divine Other. Collective unity was produced through submission, or dependence, of that sort. It was a very hierarchized, vertical system in which all individuals merged and became one with the community under the auspices of radical transcendence. With modernity, we switch to a different mode of structuration, an *autonomous* mode of structuration. Individuals now give themselves their own laws to govern the polity; the reference to transcendence gives way to this new immanence of politics. To put it very roughly, previously, power descended from above; now it rises from below. It is now conceived of as an emanation and a representation of society itself. In concrete terms, this means the rise of parliamentarianism in traditionally monarchical regimes, through the implementation of "universal" suffrage (limited to men only at first, and for a very long time thereafter . . .). From heteronomy to autonomy: this is the interpretation of modernity that I propose as an alternative to the Marxist interpretative frame of history.

Now, at a very specific moment of this transition – in the late nineteenth century, to be precise – radical doubt arose about the project of modernity. The gradual shift to autonomy held out a promise of unity. But what actually happened? A host of new divisions developed. The democratic societies seemed to be torn by irreducible divisions. This was a far cry from the ideal picture conjured up by the philosophers who were beacons of modernity. Rousseau, the very inventor of the notion of autonomy, imagined that the social contract would lead to collective harmony, that the relationships between contracting individuals would be based on political reciprocity. But, in actual fact, no such thing happened: representation created a distance from the people, the specter of hierarchy and heteronomy returned, insofar as the few continued to speak for the many, and the "average" citizen did not really see him/herself as the creator of the law, contrary to what was implied by the concept of general sovereignty. The liberal thinkers, for their part, announced that the market economy would unite individual interests and propel society as a whole toward prosperity. In actual fact, the growth of capitalism brought about class antagonisms and gross inequalities. In short, the experience of modernity was painful. It seemed to doom democracy to impossibility.

What relationship developed between these impasses of autonomy and the advent of totalitarianisms?

M.G.: The answer to that is almost in the question! In the late nineteenth century, in the face of divided societies that seemed increasingly unsustainable in the long term, the only sensible project was to resort to unity. The challenge was to restore the inner workings of the old religious totality and to do so within disputed modernity itself. This general aspiration would give rise to two powerful illusions, which were convergent but distinct. In one case, it was a matter of *restoring* the collective unity that was considered to be lost or buried. This was a fundamentally reactionary project, swallowed up by the past, and which would be carried by the fascist and Nazi totalitarianisms. In the other case, the stated objective was to *bring about* that unity, to create a society that would be beyond divisions. The project was essentially revolutionary, future-oriented. Marxism supplied the internal software, and it was Russian totalitarianism that would ultimately take charge of it.

Thus, fascism, Nazism, and communism amounted to *secular religions*: or how to recreate a community and transcendence within modern immanence. Of course, those involved didn't have a clear awareness of the true nature of their enterprise. It was historical analysis that brought to light the unthought elements, the conditions of possibility of totalitarian regimes – the background from which they can emerge. On the basis of relatedness, however, the methods of achieving the objectives were reversed. In the case of fascism or Nazism, the project of restoring heteronomy (complete domination over society) was achieved by using the "means" of autonomy (via the nation-state forms and the plebiscitary leader, Mussolini or Hitler). In the Soviet case, the project of bringing about autonomy (the project of a self-organizing society) was achieved by using the "means" of heteronomy (through the state's total domination over society). It was this surreptitious reintroduction of heteronomy that we witnessed starting with Lenin, but this aspect wasn't identified and conceived of as such at the time it was occurring. As they arise from an unnatural alliance between autonomy and heteronomy, totalitarianisms are monstrous, inevitably doomed to self-destruction. These phenomena are almost like political schizophrenia. Such regimes are plagued with a madness that can nevertheless be rationally explained once they're put back in the context of a broader historical experience.

Alain Badiou, to what extent does the similarity between totalitarian regimes seem relevant to you? And what do you think about Marcel Gauchet's concept of secular religion?

A.B.: I certainly won't deny that there are common elements between them. The similar features are patently obvious: in each case, the despotism of a single party, the crucial role of the political police, the pervasiveness of the military imaginary (all the political officials in communist states wore military uniforms in those years), the systematic use of terror against opponents, or even against some supporters, and so on. I'd simply add another source for comparison, one that has to do with the historical origins of these regimes. Ultimately, they all emerged from the same crisis: the tragic crisis of the imperial parliamentarianisms that was World War I, which was experienced as an almost incomprehensible pathology, as a suicide of civilized Europe. Resentment against the parliamentary democracies colored much of what happened in the USSR and Germany. In both those countries there developed a particularly vengeful climate, conducive to outbreaks of violence. I would remind you that Russia had to sign the Treaty of Brest-Litovsk in 1918 under very shameful conditions and that Germany felt that it was the great injured party of the Treaty of Versailles.

M.G.: And Italy was in a way the big loser of the victory . . .

A.B.: Exactly, the Italians were the losers of the apparent triumph. But you know, no one was really the "winner" of the Great War. It was a universal catastrophe. So here we have a common historical matrix. Can we now go one step further in linking the totalitarianisms? I think the concept of totalitarianism is justifiable and useful on one condition: that we assume its purely formal character, which cuts us off from the effective reality of its historical deployment. In logic, one formal structure can generate two models that are completely different in every respect and are not formalized in the structure in question. That's what happened in this instance. However much we might look for and identify a formal kinship between them, Nazism and communism, I repeat, differ dramatically when it comes to the values promoted, the subjectivities involved, and the global significance of their ambition.

M.G.: Once again, I don't want to dumb down the analysis! The particular danger of the category of "totalitarianism" is precisely the dissolving of differences. That's why it needs to be used with caution. Otherwise, you end up with outrageous statements, irresponsible nonsense, in which the logic of crude equation is working overtime. In this case, the danger would be to neglect the differences you pointed out. From the outset, Nazism was all about identity, with the superiority of the Aryan race that Hitler proclaimed right from the start. Later, the aim would be to universalize this particularity by working to ensure its worldwide domination. This "universalist" dimension of Nazism is not always noted ... With Leninism and, later, Stalinism, the exact opposite approach was followed: the logic was certainly internationalist at first, but it would be realized with means that amounted to a kind of particularism, insofar as the USSR's foreign policy was characterized by typically imperialistic reflexes. The regime would gradually absorb the East European countries into its sphere of influence. Nazism and communism therefore evolved in opposite ways.

My aim is to examine such differences closely and at the same time identify an underlying, shared political framework. Another, diametrically opposed danger would be simply to say there's no connection at all . . . The concept of secular religion allows me to identify a comprehensive profile of totalitarian regimes beyond or beneath the outward opposition.

A.B.: I was coming to that . . . As someone who's a staunch atheist, although I'm often accused of just being a Christian philosopher in disguise, I snap to attention whenever the signifier "religion" crops up in the conversation. Concerning your phrase "secular religion," I have a first, minor reservation, of a linguistic nature. You use it to denote regimes that can be rightly condemned, rejected outright. But you should be careful not to discredit as "religious" anything that's akin to strong convictions. Today, as soon as we're presented with a really alternative model – as is communism – people froth at the mouth and call it "totalitarian." "Totalitarian" is a convenient label for immediately ruling out emancipatory politics that don't fit the model of parliamentary democracy alone. "Religion" is also the name of the process that casts suspicion on anything that undermines the dominant ideological consensus.

M.G.: May I clear myself of that suspicion? When I speak about "secular religion" it's not to discredit strong convictions and beliefs – I much prefer the term "beliefs" to the meaningless, empty one of "values." Human beings are so constituted that they can only function with beliefs. It's entirely possible that beliefs can be strong without being religious. Nor is it a question of pitting a regime of strong conviction, which would be essentially religious, against a regime of weak conviction, which would be fundamentally secular. In "secular religion," "religion" denotes a very precise content, which refers to the idea of transcendence.

A.B.: OK, I exonerate you and will move on to my "strong" objection, in fact. It's on a more historical and conceptual level. With your notion of "secular religion," your focus is on a fusional description of past, so-called "totalitarian" societies. They're supposedly placed unequivocally under the sign and the law of the One. Their aim is a great communion. At the beginning of the conversation you were already suggesting that Lenin had taken over a latent totalitarian dimension from Marx, with the idea of a society reconciled and free of its divisions . . .

M.G.: Yes, and I have no problem repeating that: Marx reformulated the communist idea in materialistic terms, even if his materialism was more of a point of honor with him than a true philosophical logic. His thinking purported to be very down-to-earth, pragmatic. He advocated the elimination of all barriers internal to society. In a way, that leads to totalitarianism, to the law of the One, in fact. But of course, make no mistake about it: it's not an automatic transition! I don't claim that Marxism necessarily leads to totalitarianism. I don't want to prejudge as such what might be considered the intrinsically totalitarian dimension of the communist idea. Nevertheless, Marx's version of it makes possible, provides the deep root of, a totalitarian interpretation of the sort that Lenin would make a reality.

A.B.: That hypothesis about Marx's thought seems quite risky to me, just as your analysis of historical communism seems ultimately unfeasible and strikes me as having only polemical value.

M.G.: The differences between us are becoming clearer . . .

A.B.: Let's look at what actually happened. Let's take the historical distance you yourself attach such importance to. In reality, what did Lenin do? Anything but create a unified society! He continued to maintain, and even increased, certain divisions and factors of inequality. For example, on the question of the organization of work, he studied Taylorism closely and in fact reinforced discipline and hierarchical divisions. He constantly emphasized the power and competence of experts, the distinguished masters of the science of history. Naturally, he declared that the country had to move boldly forward to mechanize the countryside; at no time, however, was there an intrinsic process of reduction or elimination of the differences between the cities and the rural areas. As for the state apparatus, it was neither weakened nor done away with but on the contrary made stronger. After Lenin, Stalin himself never portrayed Soviet society as a unified totality. Quite the contrary! He said that, under socialism, class struggle had not only continued to exist but had actually grown more intense. In short, the basic scenario in the USSR was not at all totalizing or unified. The real decisions that were made were not in line with what you've described.

In China too, profound obstacles and distinctions remained or were created. Before the Cultural Revolution, the very strict distinction between engineers and workers in the factories was reaffirmed on the basis of the Soviet model. Liu Shaoqi, the president of the People's Republic of China from 1959 to 1968, stressed the importance of both the individual bonus system and the retention of the possibility of laying off workers in the interest of complying with the requirements of production imperatives. The countryside was left behind, after the big landlords were eliminated. On all these issues, at least until the early 1960s, the Chinese Communist Party followed the Stalinist line. It was precisely against these bureaucratized inequalities that Mao tried to lead an uprising, but, far from restoring a "totality," it created deep divisions in the society. This was because the philosophy of communism is dialectical through and through; it is based on the movement of contradictions, while the Nazis' philosophy was fixed in the biological reference to a "pure" essence of the people. Once again, communism and Nazism are totally different from each other. To equate them and to equate historical communism with any kind of totalizing religion strikes me as highly problematic and ultimately unjustified.

This analysis challenges your analytical framework, Marcel Gauchet. How do you account for the deepening of social differences under Lenin and Stalin, as Alain Badiou portrayed it?

M.G.: I'm not surprised; I was expecting as much! In fact, the point Alain Badiou raised, far from invalidating my interpretative hypothesis, only confirms it. Let me explain. It is indisputable that Lenin and Stalin restored and even created divisions. But it's not enough to just note them. You have to understand what logic, what dialectical process – precisely – they're inscribed in. It can never be emphasized enough, let me repeat: the Marxist-Leninist regime always presents itself as an organ of transition. It doesn't present itself as the achieved reality of history but as the point of transition that, via the established dictatorship of the proletariat, will make it possible to lead society as a whole to communism. This is a key point: the regime defines itself as a means, not an end. The divisions maintained or accentuated are part of this general framework. They're considered stages, necessary conditions for achieving communism and the unity of all the people! A present evil for a future good, in a nutshell. The differences are deepened for the very sake of the harmonious totality that always remains the regime's stated objective. To take a later example, Khrushchev, a pure Stalinist by training, still claimed to adhere to that dialectic to justify creating agro-towns, whose ultimate purpose was to eliminate the division between city and country.

Generally speaking, a widening gap emerged in the USSR between the doctrine and the effective reality. The gulf between the official discourse and the cold facts would become increasingly obvious and unbridgeable. The collective appropriation of the means of production – the iconic slogan of historical communism – was supposed to eliminate social divisions (between bosses and workers, "exploiters" and "exploited," etc.). Yet it was the opposite that happened: with the emergence of a privileged stratum of society, the bureaucracy, a new form of inequality was created. Added to this, as a second crucial phenomenon, was the absolutely irrational management of the overall production apparatus, for reasons having to do with both the circumstances and the specific kind of functioning of a centralized economy such as the USSR. Gradually, the regime found itself at odds with its basic egalitarian and "scientific" premises. The economic mismanagement and the discrepancy with respect to the goal that justified the enterprise were glaringly obvious. Given this situation, the challenge was to remain in power despite the bitter objections that reality raised to the official doctrine. The regime was constantly forced to lie about what it was in order to conceal what it was becoming. Furthermore, the Party had no solution other than to eliminate its enemies, including the "internal" ones (belonging to the state bureaucracy or even the Party apparatus itself), who saw its failings on a daily basis. Anyone who was part of the bureaucracy, either directly or indirectly, could potentially be singled out as a parasite, since this new ruling class had no legitimate existence in the regime's ideology, and, on the contrary, the ruling class was supposed to have disappeared. The double infernal spiral of lies and terror was inevitable and constantly self-perpetuating.

A.B.: I'd be inclined to agree with you on that point, which makes it possible to secularize the analysis and do without any reference to secular religion! To explain the USSR's turn toward terror, a sort of dialectical monstrosity needs to be highlighted: Marxism-Leninism, which was an invention of Stalin's, claimed to be accomplishing so-called "communist" ends with the means of a coercive state, which was in turn justified by the "temporary" need for a dictatorship of the proletariat to destroy the repressive apparatuses of the old world.

But a state communism is an oxymoron, an intolerable aberration from the point of view of Marx himself, whose basic project involved the withering away of the state and who, when it came to communist society, spoke of "free association." Marx perfectly highlighted the necessarily absurd and unrealistic nature of the idea of achieving the collective appropriation of the means of production, the construction of a new society, by a despotic state alone. To use a religious metaphor – we never change! – it's like trying to spread Christianity solely by torture and the Inquisition.

Lenin bears some responsibility for this insofar as he built the state, as I said, in the image of the militarized Party. In substance, though, he agreed with Marx. The absurdity of a communism delegated to the state is explicitly mentioned in *State and Revolution*. The book, written in 1917, directly attacks the state figure as a curse threatening the revolution and needing to be destroyed. Destruction, not just "withering away," and Lenin moreover didn't really theorize the latter term, which is nevertheless the classic one ... This position taken by Lenin was said to be only temporary, coeval with the accession to power. But at the end of his life, an extremely alarmed Lenin rose up against the dynamic of statization at the heart of the construction of the USSR. Re-read in particular the documents he had read out for him at the Party Congress in 1923. With his habitual vehemence – Stalin was very different from him personality-wise, a lot more "low key"– he denounced the state's inability to serve its original purpose. For him, the degeneration of the regime had a name, something that was preeminently to blame for it, namely the bureaucracy, which he called a pigsty. Lenin then considered – and this was an anticipation of the Maoist Cultural Revolution – the idea of controlling the state from outside, through the creation of a workers' and peasants' inspectorate and through the revival of "extra-Party" popular organizations. These were projects that were extremely difficult to carry out, as he himself acknowledged.

I'm recalling this in honor of Lenin, that's all. To be sure, under Stalin, the state's stranglehold steadily increased. The regime concluded that the only option was terrorist radicalism – I don't shy away from using that term, as I've never been a Stalinist or a member of the French Communist Party – with the endless purges that resolved none of the vital problems of socialist construction. As is always the case with episodes of revolutionary deadlock, terror was considered to be the sole temporary remedy that could maintain the illusion that they were doing what they claimed to be achieving, even as the impossibilities and aporias became increasingly flagrant. At any rate, the Idea is inevitably perverted once the transition to communism has been entrusted to the state alone. The lesson moreover goes beyond the exemplary, instructive case of the Stalinist state.

How so?

A.B.: To my mind, every state possesses an inherent criminal dimension, because *every* state is a mixture of violence and conservative inertia. When its message no longer resonates, once the moment of enthusiasm that accompanies the revolutionary establishment of a new power is past, when its incompetence and its inertia are patent, it always attempts to forge ahead. The state is an entity that has only one idea: to persevere in its being, as Spinoza would say. It will stop at nothing to stay in place, and anyone opposing it had better watch out. The state is the very opposite of genuine politics. Adherence to the state or the party always produces an effect of subjective depoliticization. We've seen many examples of this, such as the "official" communist militants at the orders of the general secretary, brainwashed, incapable of thinking for themselves without *L'Humanité* [the official newspaper of the French Communist Party] ready to hand ... Every politics worthy of the name must necessarily express its disagreement with, its principled independence from, the various forms of statist omnipotence and persistence.

Conversely, this is what I found in Mao: the idea that "the communist movement," as he called it, cannot be left to the state apparatus, that it's necessary for independent mass movements, and even people's organizations separate from the Party, to be created in the dynamic of history, even if need be in the form of the uprising.

M.G.: Before we get into the supposed exception of Maoism, I'd like to point out the fact that your explanation of totalitarianism, inspired by the internal criticisms that Stalinism was subjected to early on within the communist movement itself, strikes me, almost a century after the original event of the revolution of 1917, as being surprisingly limited. Because you rather quickly sidestep something essential, which all the writers who've investigated these regimes have focused attention on. I'd even go so far as to say that it's here that you overlook something essential within historical communism: the properly political logic of terror. You explain the "perversion" of communism by the fact that it merged with the state: captured by the logic of domination characteristic of state institutions, but also by historical contingencies particular to each of the countries where it tried to become established, the "wonderful" communist project supposedly went astray. But really, Alain Badiou, state domination is several thousand years old, as you well know, whereas totalitarianism, regardless of whether it's the fascist, Nazi, or communist version of it, is a completely new phenomenon ... Your analysis fails to take account of the specificity of totalitarianism as compared with all the political regimes of the past. Because there is really a logic of terror operating in the enthusiasm of all the communist movements, from Stalin's Russia to Mao's China to Castro's Cuba or Pol Pot's Cambodia: no regime, whatever you may think, was able to do without terror. A very special kind of terror, which was not related only to the existence of the state but seemed to be endogenous to the communist project itself. In the guise of enemies of the people, all social classes, from intellectuals to Party members to any Tom, Dick, or Harry, could be singled out as an enemy agent. That's something that can't be explained satisfactorily by relating it exclusively to the state and has to do with the totalitarian dimension of the communist project as such: with the idea you reject, namely that communism aims to dissolve all activities and differences in the One. That said, I'm particularly curious to know how you think the Maoist regime was an exception to the rule ...

Alain Badiou, it would certainly be useful here for you to clarify the meaning of your constantly reaffirmed commitment to Maoism, which has often sparked controversy . . . How is it still possible to profess allegiance to Mao, whose name is associated with a regime of infamous memory?

A.B.: When it comes to my fidelity to Maoism, you really have to understand what you're talking about. It's so easy to caricature it . . . I haven't retained everything from Mao. In some respects there was an indisputable continuity between the Chinese and Stalinist regimes. I'm thinking in particular of the inordinate power acquired by the bureaucratic class. But that's a lineage I dismiss out of hand. What I'm mainly concerned with is the Cultural Revolution. This very poorly understood revolutionary episode went through several very different stages. I only focus on its beginning sequence, the initial phase that began in 1966, reached its high point in 1967, and can be considered as being over by fall 1968 at the latest. This first sequence represented an enterprise with a unique political content: what we witnessed was the first authentically communist mass movement. Mao launched an unprecedented appeal, which undermined Stalinism from within. He sparked an enormous mobilization, first of students, then of workers. The source of change was no longer the state or the Party; rather, it was drawn from social forces that, although unorganized at first, were considered as the only true actors of historical and political creation. This marked the only attempt in the history of communism to challenge the tragic outcome of the experience of Soviet socialism, namely, the capture of politics by the state. When the state, via the Party, gains a monopoly on political action it leads in actual fact to a total depoliticization of society. Totalitarianism is sometimes defined as a regime in which everything becomes political. I, for one, think it should be defined instead as an eradication of politics. That's what Mao wanted to break with. When, before an audience of Red Guards, who were enthralled by the figure of the political leader, Mao said: "Get involved in the affairs of the state," it was a gesture absolutely contrary to the entire Stalinist heritage.

Of course, the mobilization failed, owing to its internal breakdown, its lack of discipline and organization, the factional struggles it caused, and the fierce resistance of the mid-level cadres of the Party apparatus. It's not a question of fetishizing the GPCR (the "Great Proletarian Cultural Revolution," as it was called back then). In terms of the experiment it represented, however, the promise of the Maoist revolution was huge, and its legacy decisive.

M.G.: Yes, but we're talking about a venture whose criminal dimension it would be a mistake to underestimate. By the most historically serious estimates, the number of victims during the period of the Cultural Revolution alone was between 750,000 and 1,500,000!

A.B.: I'm familiar with that "objection." The death count is the zero dimension of political polemics. Regarding the Cultural Revolution, people become outraged before they understand. The range you mentioned is too broad to be authoritative, and it concerns the entire revolutionary process of more than 10 years. Seven hundred fifty thousand dead over a period of 10 years, on the scale of

China, I'm sorry to have to say this . . . but if you applied that type of calculation to the French Revolution, including the Vendée uprising, you'd end up with figures that weren't so different, relatively speaking. I don't think you'd derive a definitive critique of the republican form of state from them! How can anyone imagine that a struggle for a total reorientation of power, for a complete overhaul of the form of the state itself, could be accomplished without substantial material and human damage? When parliamentary democracies, which are still your political fetish, Marcel Gauchet, are called on to take responsibility for large-scale atrocities – as happened with them at the time of colonial wars and global conflicts, where it was a matter of deaths by the tens of millions – do you conclude that these democracies are essentially criminal regimes? No, clearly you don't draw that sort of conclusion. Mao was in charge of a complex, multifaceted venture, which, although locally violent, was much less so than the commonly used statistics suggest. For example, we now know that one of the decisive episodes of the first sequence, "the Wuhan episode," in July 1967, caused the death of a little fewer than a thousand people. That's a lot, but it's not on the scale of the maximal figures circulating in public opinion.

M.G.: You're counting now, too . . . The work of historians cannot be challenged in such an offhand and ideologically biased way. It's frankly irresponsible to reduce the heart of the Cultural Revolution to a single event that supposedly caused only a few hundred deaths.

A.B.: My intention was certainly not to minimize losses like those! You just have to be wary of the assessments

---

put forward by adversaries. Where did most of the violence that occurred during the Cultural Revolution actually come from? From the clashes between factions and from their anarchistic actions, as is seen in all revolutions. We should note in this respect that the most fanatic people were the rightwing Red Guard groups who supported the regime and were composed largely of children of cadres, whose objective was to defend their privileges. That said, most of the violence, particularly from the 1970s on, came from the explicitly anti-Maoist action of the army and the state apparatus, which gave the orders to fire on the revolutionaries everywhere, especially in the provinces, in order to regain control. Where the Maoist left was strong, as in Shanghai, organizing workers and students in a new, flexible framework, under the direction of experienced, inventive political leaders, there were very few deaths. Conversely, where the bureaucratic and military right was very powerful, as in Canton, the violence was extreme. This reminds me of the fact that the heaviest-loaded cart bound for the guillotine in 1794 was not of Robespierre's doing but of the counter-revolutionary Thermidoreans', who were beginning a long period of White Terror by executing all the leaders of the great Committee of Public Safety.

M.G.: I grant you that the complexity of the Cultural Revolution has been generally glossed over. You remain on the level of pure politics rather than on that of statistics. The pill, so to speak, may seem hard to swallow, but fine, let's adopt that perspective. Well, on this same level, I would come back at you with the fact that Mao was certainly not the anti-Stalin. He didn't evince that singularity of proposing a "different," more "authentic" communism. You argue that the Cultural Revolution possessed an extra-totalitarian dimension during its opening phase. Those who have since studied that event thoroughly have arrived at a completely different interpretation. Mao drew all the logical conclusions from the Soviet regime, and his leadership was entirely consistent with Stalinism. What he did at the start of the Cultural Revolution was highly reminiscent of what happened in the USSR in 1936–8. Those were the years of the most appalling terror. Yet at that precise moment, and it's anything but coincidental, Stalin was already seeking to form an alliance with the masses. He involved them directly in the drafting of the famous Soviet "most democratic constitution in the world" – a pure propaganda tool, inasmuch as that constitution wasn't meant to be applied . . . The popular mobilization was the means for justifying the ongoing purges. It was all about forging an alliance between the people and the top level of political power, and it was formed in opposition to the mid-level Party apparatus . . .

A.B.: . . . mid-level or pretty high up, since it went all the way up to the Political Bureau of the Party itself.

M.G.: Exactly, it was a gangrene phenomenon. Even at the highest levels of the Party there was a rush to finger traitors, saboteurs, rogues, enemies of the cause, and so on. And they would be dealt with accordingly. Mao's intention was similar: he resisted the bogging down of his own regime by deliberately appealing to the popular masses of a specific sort, namely, the well-educated youth. That's possibly the only way in which he was original: Stalin would certainly not have imagined using such a recourse ... Nevertheless, the overall strategy was the same. All the communist regimes ended up with internal contradictions that led to this spiral: the regime turned against itself and reaffirmed its legitimacy with the masses – but only in order to regenerate itself, not to change. The Party attacked the Party: terror was logically involved in this process, so the psychological analyses that attempt to account for it (they mention Stalin's paranoia, Mao's megalomania, and so on) are pointless. No, it was a properly political mechanism that was set in motion. It was the system itself that was paranoid! To come back to the Cultural Revolution and to sum up my remarks, Mao merely repeated a "classically" Stalinist and typically totalitarian gesture, I'm sorry to have to say ...

Chapter 4
The return of the communist hypothesis?

Twenty-five years ago, the Berlin Wall fell. The Communist bloc collapsed, and the liberal-democracy model seems to have definitively prevailed. Alain Badiou, why do you think that the failure of the communist experiment doesn't invalidate the very idea that served as its foundation? And how might communism rise from its ashes today?

Alain Badiou: I maintain that the historical experience of communism, which was incidentally multifaceted and fragmented, does not provide a conclusive argument against the Idea itself. There's no reason to turn that experience into a historical trial of the communist perspective. We're talking about a sequence that extends roughly from 1917 to 1989. Seventy years: that's much shorter than the Spanish Inquisition, which also used means that were incompatible with Christian belief but has never been considered, as far as I'm aware, as an experience that wholly and definitively encompassed and discredited that religion. History can't be used to disqualify the Idea forever.

My approach involves distinguishing between three stages. There's the communism of the nineteenth century, when the Idea was formulated, by Marx and others. There's the communism of the twentieth century, when, having been put into practice under state control, it was tenuous or distorted. We need to write our own assessment of this perversion, and the lesson to be learned from such an error can be summed up in one sentence: communism is an Idea that's too grand to be entrusted to a state. As Marx himself said, the overall disposition of communism is incompatible with the methods, existence, and development of a state power that is moreover militarized and despotic due to its insurrectional, revolutionary, and violent origins. Finally, there's the third stage of the periodization: a new sequence, still in its infancy, is beginning in the early years of the twenty-first century. We're at a crossroads, in a period of great ferment that's strongly reminiscent of the late 1840s. In this general context, as often happens, a very big step backward is needed in order to make a new leap forward. This means going back to the original communism and salvaging the basic characteristics of the Idea itself so as to adapt it appropriately to the modern world. Now more than ever, we can, we must, and we will reactivate the communist hypothesis.

How is the word "hypothesis" being used by you?

A.B.: As I already mentioned, a great deal of my culture is scientific. I give the word "hypothesis" a technical meaning, similar to the one it has in epistemology. A hypothesis, in this instance, isn't a more or less fanciful assumption of the mind, a more or less credible invention of the imagination. No, I mean "hypothesis" in the experimental sense, as a general scheme of thought that can give rise to concrete experiences and can thus be gradually embodied and verified. This meaning is closely akin to another part of my culture, my militant commitment. The communist hypothesis thus refers to the possibility and testing out of a scheme provided by the Idea – the communist Idea.

We get it now . . . So what would your current definition of communism be?

A.B: Let me begin by mentioning three components of a generic definition. First, "communism" is the name of the conviction that it's possible to extricate the becoming of all humanity from the evil grip of capitalism. The still absolutely critical importance of private property, the uncontrolled interplay of competing interests, the frantic pursuit of profit as the sole law of economic activity, the diktats of economic and financial monopolies: all this has spawned inequalities as undeniable as they are monstrous. We were talking about the pathological nature of "totalitarian" societies, but isn't the current neoliberal world just as pathological? Today, 10 percent of the world's population possesses 86 percent of the resources. One percent of the world's population owns 46 percent of those same resources. Those are the official figures, and they will continue to grow. Is a world like that tolerable? No. Accepting it is out of the question. Freeing the collective space from capital's pernicious control would be the first level of the definition. Second, "communism" denotes the hypothesis that the state, a coercive apparatus distinct from society but allowed by it into its existence and reproduction, is not a natural, inevitable form of the structuration of human societies. We can and we must do without it. This is related to the notion of the withering away of the state in the classical Marxist tradition. Third, "communism" means that the division of labor (with the divisions it implies between tasks of execution and management, between manual and intellectual labor, and so on) is in no way an absolute necessity for organizing economic production.

When combined, these three points make up a comprehensive alternative to the development of human history up to the present. Thus, "communism" will denote the possibility and pursuit of the unification, in a real historical process, of these three dimensions: the deprivatization of the production process, the withering away of the state, and the reunification and polymorphism of labor.

Isn't a definition like that entirely consistent with Marx and Marxism?

A.B: Yes, in a way, it's an orthodox definition. I'm reminding you of these points of definition because they've been forgotten today or because they're considered to be purely theoretical ...

Marcel Gauchet: Those points are basic, of course, but they've actually never really been well known!

A.B.: We agree. We've got to get back to basics ... After defining the Idea, I will now turn to the issue of communist organization itself. Indeed, the combination of the three points I mentioned is rooted in real practice. The communist hypothesis is carried by a collective subject that could not be more real: those we'll call "communists." I intentionally maintain a certain vagueness about the concrete identity of this collective subject. In the Marxist tradition it corresponds to the proletariat. In the Maoist tradition the communist subject is embodied in the masses, which can't be reduced to just the working class: Mao sometimes defined the proletariat as "all the friends of the revolution," which is a subjective and biased conception, to say the least! But, to my mind, we shouldn't make an a priori judgment about the nature of the actors who support the communist Idea; the collective subject must be able to take on a number of possible forms.

On the question of its organization, I'll return to Marx again. I believe four teachings that are equivalent to criteria can be deduced from his thinking. First of all, Marx developed an idea that was very important, indeed fundamental, in my opinion: according to him, communists aren't "outsiders," they're not a distinct or isolated historical and political component. On the contrary, they're directly involved in a pre-existing general movement that they'll later be responsible for directing. Communists must assert their difference but without cutting themselves off from the general dynamic that makes their very existence possible. That immediately precludes their grouping together as a separate vanguard, or a party operating in a vacuum. With Mao, that principle became a sort of definition of politics, under the name of "the mass line." In Mao's view, the Party was nothing if it was not completely immersed in the popular movement from which it derived its existence as well as its programmatic and tactical ideas. I gradually became opposed to the idea of a "communist party" in the traditional sense, because I think every party points to a core group, a pattern of authority, which leads back to an authoritarian negation and eradication of multiplicity. The transcendence of the One is always re-established in the figure of the Party. The One is my main enemy, however, both metaphysically and politically. But please don't misunderstand me: I'm not advocating anarchistic disorganization. The point I'm making is that we need to find coherent and effective forms of intervention, which, although connected to society, go beyond the party model.

The basic concept is less that of leadership than of direction. Indeed, this is the second criterion: the bearers of the communist Idea are characterized by an ability to communicate what the next step is. This is a tactical issue in that communists are responsible for saying what the immediate future might look like. It's not their job to present great rapturous scenes of the coming paradise or to hold forth at every opportunity on the ideal society that may never come to pass . . . Let's leave that to utopians of all persuasions. No, communists must define what political forms are possible with regard to the current situation. If there's a failure to present a credible picture of the next step, then every revolutionary movement will lead to a dead end. To give but one example, look at what happened in Egypt recently. The leaders of the admirable uprising of 2011 had no idea where they were headed. People who don't know what they want invariably demand "democratic" elections. These elections, as usual, bring to power people whom the revolutionaries of the first hour don't like, in this case the Muslim Brotherhood. So the revolutionaries took to the streets again against the Brotherhood. And, using this divided uprising as a pretext, the military, the longstanding enemy of the Brotherhood, launched a coup d'état and took back power – the military power against which the young revolutionaries had risen up to the cries of "Mubarak, get out!" It was a sort of circular movement all for nothing. This is why there's a need to really visualize the end result of the revolutionary movement, to anticipate what is coming, to refrain from simple negative impulses, and that's a basic responsibility of communist politics.

The third criterion of communist organization is that it must follow an internationalist logic. Marx stressed this point heavily, and that's why he created the First International. But once again, internationalism must not harden into a separate entity. Communists are internationalists, but they must be so right within the local processes of emancipation. They must not think in terms of contingent or limited (national, regional, etc.) interests but understand the universal contribution of their action: what happens here concerns the whole world. And finally, the fourth and last criterion, communists must defend a global strategic vision, subsumed by the Idea as I have presented it, and whose matrix is anti-capitalism.

There, now combine the generic definition (in three points) and the "organizational" definition (in four points) and you'll get what I mean by "communism." A real political program in seven points!

M.G.: Like in the good old days! But tell me: do you really think today's working classes are converting to this new communist program? I, for one, don't see any sign of that . . .

A.B.: Don't be ironic. I've taken part in many international discussions about the word "communism," first in London, then in Berlin and New York, and last year in South Korea. We will continue. These initiatives pool many new political experiences throughout the world. When you see how loads of people – many of whom are involved in local struggles and organizations – come to hear us and interact productively with us, you should take that as a beginning, as yet very modest, no doubt, but real, of verification of what matters to me: the Idea and its development in reality.

Marcel Gauchet, Alain Badiou gave a detailed explanation of the meaning of his revival of the communist idea today. What's your reaction to the international success of this revitalization?

M.G.: The meeting of minds, even of a great many of them, around the communist idea is by no means a beginning of verification of the hypothesis itself. It's a verification of the *appeal* the hypothesis exerts. That's not the same thing! I can completely understand the appeal. I'm not blind. Like you, I see the deleterious effects of capitalism today. And, like you, I think it would be terrible to become resigned, to give up the hope of a profound transformation of the world. If consent to what currently exists were to dominate unilaterally it would strike me as an unprecedented intellectual and moral tragedy. That those who suffer from the consequences of capitalism should aspire to a better society seems absolutely legitimate and noble to me. But the nobility of the cause is not a guarantee of the correctness of the approach. It can even act as a smokescreen.

There's something that strikes me about the proponents of the communist hypothesis: they, like you, Alain Badiou, have a sort of aristocratism about them that seems like a political impasse to me. The far left today strongly reminds me of the conscious vanguard of the revolutionary parties that had so turned me off in my youth. It presents itself as a sort of enlightened nobility operating in the pure realm of Ideas, like an insider elite whose main motivation is to mark its supreme difference from the way things are. Psychologically, it can feel good to feel different or out of the ordinary. But in practice it has absolutely no effect! I had occasion to say this elsewhere, but I think radicalism is often a pose. I'm not talking about genuine intellectual radicalism, which consists in going to the root of problems. I'm talking about politically expedient radicalism, which consists in outdoing yourself in your opposition to the world as it is. This has many benefits. First, it lets you reap the symbolic benefits of radicalism without having to pay the price in the form of real work. The pose replaces the content and becomes an end in itself. Second, you attain moral authenticity by refusing any compromise with the established order. You're in the right in the present, and at the same time you're privy to the future – a sleight of hand that indicates a collapse and a regrettable eradication of all political intelligence.

In the end, the pose of radicalism in no way destabilizes what it purports to challenge. It's fashionable, and you can show off in public discussions and lecture to overflow audiences on elite campuses, but it's useless. Nothing concrete can be expected from it. Truth be told, the communist hypothesis strikes me as being typically imbued with the values of . . . capitalism, of the media-mercantile climate we're steeped in. It works like an attractive brand name, a company label that gives its followers what Bourdieu would have called . . .

A.B.: . . . a distinction?

M.G.: Right, you're suggesting the word to me yourself!

A.B.: You make it sound as though the intellectuals who support communism are a bunch of reckless, irresponsible dreamers, out of touch with the realities of the contemporary world. That's a largely mistaken view and a fantasy itself. You see, you have to look at what we do, otherwise you engage in groundless attacks. Let me give you an example. So in October 2013 – this is recent – we went to South Korea to discuss communism. There were some fascinating talks on the current, real situation of the proletariat in China. Hundreds of thousands of men and women are transported almost forcibly from the countryside to the cities and are treated horribly: they're like nomads of the interior, whose movement is controlled according to extremely stringent standards. There really are such people! Did you know that the Apple corporation alone employs 1,400,000 Chinese workers in its factories in China? Incidentally, that definitively undercuts the idea that workers are disappearing. In actual fact, there have never been so many workers in the world. This is an overwhelming fact that can't be ignored, which I got to know about on the ground, not at dinner parties! In South Korea, after the conference, we visited a working-class town that was almost entirely devoted to making inexpensive furniture. We were able to speak at length there with migrant workers who came from Bangladesh or Nepal for the most part. They provide a very precise picture of capitalist exploitation ... We mentioned a project that they were very interested in: starting an international journal of the world proletariat. Testimonies would be collected in this journal: the words of a Malian worker would "come into contact with" those of a Nepalese worker, and so on. If I'm mentioning this trip to Korea and these initiatives it's to show that I don't just toss the communist Idea around in an abstract way. Not at all.

That's how I imagine the role of intellectuals and philosophers in all this: we communists have to work to combine the theoretical aspect of the Idea with local actions that can embody it, by creating a new political subjectivity, which is still only latent today, in the potential participants in these actions. The foremost political task is to work toward the combination of four forces that are currently distinct from one another. There's the portion of the educated, university-trained youth, characterized by their desire to challenge the dominant order. There's the dissident working-class youth, who live on the outskirts of cities in our countries, or who are rising up all over the world, in Arab, Latin American, or Asian countries. There's the international nomadic proletariat, who are already involved in revolts against existing work conditions – violent strikes break out every day in China, and we know that the phenomenon is spreading across all of Asia and the whole world. Last but not least, there's the least well-established segment

of ordinary employees in our "comfortable" societies, who are hit by the job insecurity and uncertainty
brought on by financial crises. All these different actors
can gradually be brought together and united around
the communist Idea, which can give meaning and purpose to their disparate aspirations. If they're no longer
separated, these forces will be the source and driving
force of the third sequence of communism that's beginning. It will be based on types of political engagement
and organization that I can't anticipate but which I hope
will get us out of the usual circuits, the traditional political channels. The stakes are much higher than whether
we'll win the next election or whether we'll succeed in
infiltrating one city council or another. So, sure, it's a
long process, but it's already occurring on the ground
– not in the "pure realm of Ideas," to use your phrase,
which is aimed at me as an admirer of Plato . . .

**Just so we're clear, what fundamental objection do
you, Marcel Gauchet, have to the position held by your
opposite number?**

M. G.: Let's get things straight. In terms of its intellectual purity, the communist idea doesn't bother me
in the least. It's unquestionably one of the most important ideas anyone can have about the economic and
political organization of collective life. It is the heir
to the modern project, differing in that respect from
the reactionary enterprises represented by fascism and
Nazism in the twentieth century. The emphasis on the
common, the promotion of the egalitarian imperative: I
fully endorse all of that in theory. The communist idea
seems much more congenial to me than a certain other

pure idea of politics – because there's not just one idea, Alain Badiou, there are at least two! – namely, the anarchist idea, the conception of a society made up only of sovereign individuals coexisting totally independently and separately. I note, moreover, that contemporary societies in the West are inclined far more toward this anarchist idea than to the one you defend. Apart from my initial reservation about its proponents' pose, I can completely understand the power of attraction the communist idea exerts. But the problem begins when attempts are made to apply it in practice. I can't go along with that. Rejuvenate the communist idea? Sure, why not? Try to make it come back down to solid earth? No, certainly not. That agenda is neither viable nor even desirable.

The crucial question is this: what should be done with Marx? Should we remain faithful to his agenda or give it up once and for all? The definition Alain Badiou proposes of communism is not original; it's completely classical, as he himself admits, and it matches Marx's definition overall. Listening to him, I even felt like I was reliving my youth, and I'd like to thank him for that! But today, nothing seems more dangerous to me than entertaining the idea that applied Marxism, as it was embodied in history, is an abomination, while fundamental Marxism is true for all eternity. And that's more or less what the communist hypothesis encourages us to do. Even apart from its political consequences, Marx's thought should be examined as to its truth value. On a number of crucial points, however, it is seriously wrong. First of all, Marx locks us into the idea of the primacy of economics, the idea that humanity's trajectory is ultimately determined by the different modes of production through which people regulate their relations with nature and among themselves. That was an idea that seemed inspired to me at the beginning but is actually just plain false. We need to extricate ourselves from that obsessive method of interpretation and replace it with an approach that, on the contrary, downplays the role of economics – it's not a question of ignoring economics or denying its significance but of challenging its predominance in the explanation of how societies function. Second, Marx's thought goes astray in terms of its vision of what a society without a state might be, as well as in terms of the theory of history it proposes. It is in thrall to the scientific model – just like your "communist hypothesis," moreover, insofar as the very term "hypothesis," which was not chosen inadvertently, belongs to that register. Your term, Alain Badiou, accords very closely with a contemporary expectation focused on the need to have preconceived models to test out. It's very convenient: we're told what we should be aiming for, but, in actual fact, let the chips fall where they may . . . Here, too, we've got to slip out of the noose that Marx has placed around our necks. I think any discourse that presents itself as being under the auspices of a science of history, even a revitalized or updated one, should arouse suspicion and be combated. Because all of modern history, from the French Revolution to the twentieth century, shows that we have neither a science nor even a sufficiently strong and constituted theory of the process by which we might move toward a more satisfactory economic and social organization. The tragic excess of the communist movement in its various versions shows the failure of every ideological attempt to understand prematurely and definitively

---

how a society works. Reality constantly gives the lie to scientific pretensions, and so critical distance is imperative with regard to them. Only an understanding of societies that has shed the scientistic paradigm will allow us to develop a will capable of moving them in the direction we think is the right one. That is a rule of a non-Marxist method: we should beware of ready-to-use models; instead, we should closely examine what really happens, and, on the basis of that analysis, try to make a difference. The tension between the spontaneous dynamic of history and the will we can develop to influence it is our condition.

A. B.: We haven't gotten to the crux of the argument yet, I can tell, but I would nevertheless like to comment on this first part of it. I've never been, either now or in the past, a blind disciple of Marx, or even a "Marxist." Just as with Mao, my appreciation of Marx is selective, linked to the political circumstances and my intellectual interests. I readily admit my share of orthodoxy, if only to provide grist for the anti-totalitarian professionals' mill, but my Marxisant filiation isn't relevant to the two points you just mentioned. First let's say that the idea of society being completely determined by economics has never been my natural element. That thesis functions more often than not as an authoritarian intellectual method, which immediately limits the possibilities both theoretically and practically.

Furthermore, you correctly note Marx's constant reference to science. I, for one, see nothing positive to be gained from the supposedly scientific nature of Marxism-Leninism. The idea that there's something like a science of history serves as an intellectual or ideological smokescreen for the monolithic nature of state power. It's so easy to proclaim that science, like religion before it – see, Marcel Gauchet, I'm using your comparison! – is on the side of power! To the extent that we want to revive the communist hypothesis, it has to be uncoupled once and for all from the notion of a science of history. Why? Because science is blind to the evental dimension of things. Because it fails to recognize that the masses mounting the stage of history, as Trotsky put it, can never be programmed, that it's essentially unpredictable, incalculable. We are currently witnessing the end of the opposition between scientific and utopian communism, an opposition that played a big part in Marxism's beginnings. My position is to reject both of them. The communism I defend is the exact opposite of a utopia and yet it is in no way "scientific." It's simply one rational possibility of politics, and there are other ones, such as, for example, that of humanity's destruction as a result of the disastrous effects of globalized capitalism. This incidentally brings me into conflict with other current proponents of the communist Idea, who think that Marx gave full assurance of a becoming-communist of capitalism itself. Some persist in thinking that the historical movement is being directed, by its own law, toward communism. That's a rigid, "scientific," as it happens, vision, which history itself disproves. Marx was wrong about some things, and there's no obligation to go along with his strategic predictions.

M. G.: But you still maintain the general framework he established! You continue to think in the terms of a simplistic anti-capitalism, and you refer to "solutions" that are those of the most elementary Marxist tradition, first and foremost the collective appropriation of the means of production. For my part, I think we need to eliminate Marx's legacy for good. We won't get anywhere by making his thinking a manifesto for the present and the future. All that does is maintain the current political impotence. According to you, we should return to the purity of the communist idea of the nineteenth century, and you're betting that it can still be relevant and effective in the contemporary context. That's an unrealistic expectation, if not a philosophical mystification, because Marxism does a very poor job of explaining our globalized capitalism, not to mention the support it can attract even where its most loathsome aspects are concerned. It's not moral imprecations that will get us out of it.

A.B.: You really surprise me, because you condemn present-day capitalism but don't challenge it head-on. I can only conclude that, in spite of your reservations, you ultimately accept it. You're resigned to living in this world that nevertheless appalls you. Your position strikes me as being similar to the historian François Furet's. In *The Passing of an Illusion,* his highly questionable assessment of the Soviet experience, he wrote these uplifting lines: "The idea of *another* society has become almost impossible to conceive of, and no one in the world today is offering any advice on the subject or even trying to formulate a new concept. Here we are, condemned to live in the world as it is."[3] I knew Furet when he was a communist, so, for me, this post-

---

[3] François Furet, *The Passing of an Illusion,* tr. Deborah Furet (Chicago: University of Chicago Press, 2000), 502.

---

communist accusation is like a symptom of melancholy repudiation. Furet basically says that we should accept neoliberal society as it is and that we have to live in the world as it is, even if it fills us with despair. But wait: society is obviously what it is! Frankly, that's no big revelation! The reason given for all renunciations, all abandonments, is "reality," the world "as it is." I can't accept that the future, which has never promised anyone anything or imposed anything on anyone, should be blocked like this. Such a tautological vision of things – there's only reality, and the choice is either the capitalist liberal world or the liberal capitalist world – exhausts and debilitates the regime of possibilities. Defending this vision of things is a grave responsibility, and you defend it, Marcel Gauchet. Now more than ever, we need an expansion of possibilities. We need to have the courage to break free from the control over things imposed by the economic oligarchy, which dictates and determines everything that can or cannot be done. But we can only do so by asserting that what virtually everyone thinks is impossible is in fact possible, by arguing that something else is conceivable and can really be experienced: communism, today. How can you imagine changing the situation today without a strong, comprehensive idea, without an implacably different conception of society and the world?

M.G.: It's not the principle we differ on. I'm in complete agreement with the philosophical need to posit possibility. Saying that a political or economic model is an unsurpassable horizon never advances thinking one iota. The lines of François Furet that you quoted are certainly awkward. I knew him well and am convinced that he himself would have agreed about that. You and I condemn the same pathologies, and we share the same ambition of putting an end to them – or at least of trying to alleviate them, to contribute to their gradual destruction. Our real battlefront is elsewhere.

A.B.: And we're finally getting to it!

M.G.: So it would seem! It's very important to draw the battle lines ... Our disagreement isn't about the need to change the way things are – to change the world, as Marx would have said. It concerns the crucial question of "how." How can we do so? How can we get out of the disastrous situation we're in? As far as you're concerned, we've got to exit capitalism completely, which implies moving to its opposite, communism. To that project, which I think is irremediably doomed, I oppose a sense of caution that draws from the lessons of the past. But this cautiousness needs to be combined with the greatest audacity. In this case, audacity means saying that it's possible not to break completely with capital but to bring the economy under political control. I think we can rein capitalism in, destroy its indisputable dominance today, and do so within the democratic model, a model that needs to be completely reinvented but must be retained whatever the cost. In short, I trust the possibilities afforded by democracy itself – very great possibilities that you'd be wrong to overlook.

The battle lines have been clearly drawn now. Alain Badiou, are the democracies capable of meeting the challenge, of regaining control over capitalism?

A.B.: If we're talking about the modern form of democracy, namely, parliamentary democracy, I'm afraid this wonderful project cannot be achieved. By wanting to preserve the form, Marcel Gauchet, you underestimate a crucial point that dooms your proposition to failure: representative democracy is constitutively controlled by capital. Here, I in turn will question the very foundation of your thinking, the way you did with me when you discussed my Marxism. If I summarize the analysis you've been developing up to now, we could say that you situate totalitarianism in general, and the communist experience in particular, in the larger framework of the "exit from religion," or what Nietzsche would have called "the death of God." In Lacanian terms, it's about thinking a political enterprise that would no longer have the big Other's stamp of approval. You maintain that the pathological dimension of historical communism stems from the fact that it sought to obtain radical immanence by means of transcendence – heteronomy, in your terms – and that this resulted in a "secular religion," of which Nazism was the symmetrical opposite. This fundamental tension between autonomy and heteronomy, in your opinion, presided over the destiny of totalitarianisms, which the democracies have definitively triumphed over.

M.G.: Yes, that's what I claim, and totalitarianisms won't come back. They're dead! They're behind us, because the wellspring they drew from is gone. The fuel that would allow them to rise again has evaporated for good. This doesn't mean that we'll only have nice regimes in the future! Barbarism can appear in other guises. Nevertheless, we should give ourselves a pat on the back: the terrible tragedy of the twentieth century is over. I call for the disbanding of the anti-totalitarian troops. Their activism has been helpful, but now it's time to change fights. This is no longer the subject that should require our attention and our commitment.

A.B.: I agree with you on that point: the totalitarian-isms of the twentieth century are a historical hapax. They won't happen again. But then, sticking with your analytical framework, we are supposedly witnessing the final victory of the parliamentary democracies, all without exception situated in the globalized capital-ist context, which are the embodiment of the modern project itself. Democracy as the regime of finally pure immanence, democracy as the model that, through the mechanisms of political representation, only follows the logic of autonomy. We've supposedly finished with transcendence, with the big Other. But, for me, that's the problem, because you have to wonder whether there's not also a big Other – different from the divine big Other – lurking within representative democracy. I maintain that this big Other is capital. Capital is the big Other of democracy, which is subjected to its domi-nation and perpetuates it. It is therefore impossible to extract democratic society as we know it from the capi-talist matrix once and for all. But let me immediately add that this holds true for all time and in all places. Democracy is always linked and in thrall to capital; that's a point Marx himself had already correctly noted. As far as I know, there's no solid historical counter-example. I don't think there's ever been a parliamentary democracy anywhere but in a country where capitalism has crossed a certain threshold of development. This is what leads me to say that, one day or other, China will end up discovering the virtues of the democratic regime, which is a lot more suitable for capitalist development than the cumbersome bureaucratic system. Generally speaking, ever since the collapse of the socialist states, we've been seeing a quasi-total merging of the economic powers and the so-called political "representatives" all over the world, and this has been the case regardless of whether we're in our "democracies" or elsewhere . . .

M.G.: I don't share your analysis, which is actually deeply imbued with Marxism. Democracy can't be defined by capital's control over it. What you claim is an essential feature is in reality a statement of fact that may have seemed to be an essential feature at certain moments in the past and has a certain degree of plausibility again today. Democracy can of course resemble that profile (where it would seem to be the slave of capitalism), and, nowadays, there is no question that our leaders genuflect before the neoliberal system and go along with all the abuses it produces. Like you, I deplore this, but is it something inevitable as you suggest it is? I don't think so. To my mind, there is a fundamental independence of democracy, of the mode of organization of political life it represents, that enables it to regain control over capital. My perspective has a name: it's the path of reformism. The word arouses suspicion today; it is misused or vilified. But we need to rediscover its true meaning.

So there you have it: you, Alain Badiou, advocate a third era of the communist hypothesis, while I, on the other hand, think a third era of democratic reformism needs to begin. It's no longer a question of regulating women's and children's labor, or instituting the eight-hour work day as was done in the early twentieth century. It's no longer a question of definitively establishing French labor law and the Social Security system, as was the case after 1945. Now the issue is to regain control of the economy so as to get out of the mess we're in. This new reformist effort won't free us from capitalism. But it will make our societies better places to live in. I'm coming back to my motivating dialectic: cautiousness in the approach doesn't preclude audacity in the perspectives. But for you, I imagine, reformists are vile people . . .

A.B.: I wouldn't go that far, even if I don't think highly of them! I have a better understanding of your position, which seems idyllic to me nonetheless. Why? Because democracy, in its parliamentary form, precludes any important change. Parliamentarianism is based on the principle of power alternation, that is, on the necessary mitigation of possible sharp conflicts. This framework involves the majority political parties agreeing to make way for one another peacefully, one after the other. But that's only possible if they don't differ substantially and are ultimately in agreement about the same model of society and development. I've always thought democratic construction was based on four possible orientations. There are two government parties: one is "leftwing" and the other "rightwing." One of them – the left – defines itself as a more redistributive party than the other, but that's the only difference between them, and even then it's largely a rhetorical difference, as François Hollande's politics, a pale imitation of Nicolas Sarkozy's, show today. Second, relegated to the sidelines, there's the party representing "moderate" anti-capitalism and its various and sundry avatars, commonly called "the far left," and the party that adopts nationalistic and identitarian, or even racist, ideology, the fascist or far-right party. In this overall setup, parliamentary politics amounts to saying that state power should be entrusted to the two government parties, which, between them, actually constitute a sort of big, soft, unchanging center. That's what's called "democratic consensus," a phrase that conceals a sad reality and a glaring powerlessness: the parties called to power agree that they will ultimately not lay a hand on capital, that they'll let private property ravage the principle of the public interest. The law of parliamentary democracy is really the stifling of strong differences. Let me remind you that already at the time of the Popular Front the communists weren't allowed to be in power. In 1981 Mitterrand did of course let the communists into his government but only because he knew that the Party was already half-dead and it would be easy for him to quietly strangle it.

It always comes back to the way the GCC (the Great Consensual Center) maintains the same guiding principle. When financial and/or political crises occur, big promises are made. They tell us that our devastated society won't be done in by capital and that we're going to pull ourselves together and bring down Big Finance, which is set up as the congenital enemy. The government opposition party comes to power and trumpets its determination to reform the system from top to bottom. In practice, however, the much-vaunted reformism only results in insignificant little changes, because the leaders are actually only eager to do one thing: submit to the cult of capital again. This happens over and over, far too often for it to be merely coincidental or contingent. It's the cycle of parliamentary capitalism as such. In short, any radical opposition to capital's authority must involve a rigorous questioning of democratic "pluralism," which is merely the pluralism of nuances, of the small differences tolerated by the capitalist world.

M. G.: I believe, on the contrary, in the fruitfulness of democratic pluralism. From the experiences of totalitarianism I've drawn one very simple political rule of method, namely, the self-imposed prohibition on silencing opposition in any way whatsoever. Any different society toward which we may move will have opponents. These opponents have to be allowed to fully express and organize themselves. This doesn't stop people from having strong convictions. But the point is to put them to the test of this imperative, which, I believe, goes beyond mere healthy tolerance for the diversity of opinion. Political action must somehow include opposition. It combats it but it includes it. It can't operate otherwise. If you think about it, that's a way of operating in politics that is very different from what casual observation suggests. Indeed, the ordinary rule of liberal democracy is power alternation. This avoids having to ask fundamental questions: sometimes it's one, sometimes it's the other. All problems are resolved through moderation. But this seeming minimalism conceals an enduring capacity for invention whose resources we have only just begun to tap. The necessary inclusion of the dimension of opposition in the political process, which is the key lesson of the twentieth century, contains a remarkable capacity for renewal.

A.B.: The big problem we've inherited from the twentieth century is how to deal with the issue of enemies'
power. Like you, I believe that opposition teaches us
things and should be included. Contrary to what is often
said, I'm not a *gauchiste* or even a radical. I've always
participated in politics with the idea that we first need
to investigate, discuss, and listen to contrary views.
Anyone who immediately refuses all dialogue is a terrorist and an ignoramus. Our own discussion confirms
this general attitude of reasoned openness to difference
. . . But I think your dialectic of cautiousness and audacity fails to take sufficient account of the fact that in
any political situation there are enemies. Real, genuine
enemies. And I'm not sure the problem of enemies can
be resolved in the democratic framework as you imagine
it continuing.

**That's a strong statement . . . So what do you think
would be the right attitude to adopt toward these
enemies? Should they be included in politics, and, if so,
how can that be done if we move away from democratic
pluralism?**

A.B.: My current idea about this issue is that we need
to create conditions such that it would be up to the
enemies to decide on their position. If the enemies think
they can participate in politics, if they agree to join in
the common agora, then that opportunity should be
open to them. There's no question of excluding them
out of hand. But if they refuse to join, there's a great risk
that they may want to go on the offensive, that they may
opt for aggression. If that's the case, we'll have to defend
ourselves. Let's not be naïve: when someone attacks you

on the street the question of your immediate reaction is unavoidable. The imperative that I deduce from this is as follows: assuming that recourse to violence against enemies is necessary, it should be exclusively defensive.

What we're engaging in here, it's true, is politics-fiction, because we're still a far cry from the situation in which the enemies would have to decide. For that to happen, you'd have to imagine that a total shift in the balance of power had occurred and the communist Idea had triumphed. In the meantime, the enemies are in the majority. The capitalists are strutting their stuff! And they're much too strong to accept the far-reaching reforms you're proposing. They'll do everything in their power to oppose them, and you offer no explanation of what new means you'll have at your disposal to defeat their opposition.

M.G.: I'm not naïve. The triumph of neoliberalism is obvious and thrives on the manifest complicity of the political, economic, and intellectual spheres. I'm well aware that the type of opposition I represent is largely a minority position. You're in the same boat, incidentally . . .

A.B.: Absolutely! We both represent minority positions, and so there's no antagonism between us. Opposition, rather. Faced with the complacent majority that's so experienced in parliamentary capitalism, neither you nor I have very big troops. But here's the thing: we're both on track. You, to discover in the light of a revamped reformism a democracy in which capital would no longer be the big Other, and I, to systematize and work practically toward reactivating the communist hypothesis. The real will decide between us, assuming we're heeded.

M.G.: That way of putting it is chillingly solemn, but, all things considered, it suits me fine!

Chapter 5
What is the meaning of the crisis?

Up to now, the discussion has focused on the experience of historical communism, from which you drew different lessons. This overview of history allowed us to return to the present, and you each defined your project: a revival of the communist hypothesis, in your case, Alain Badiou, and a reformist resurgence within the democratic framework, in your case, Marcel Gauchet. Could we now examine your differences in greater detail by turning more specifically to the contemporary context? There is a widespread sense today of a pervasive crisis. It was thought that democracy had triumphed over communism, and now it seems threatened again by the turmoil capitalism is experiencing. Have we come back to a crisis comparable to the one in the 1930s? And how can democracy overcome its difficulties in the era of neoliberal globalization?

Marcel Gauchet: That's a lot of questions! And it's hard to deal with them seriously if we don't take the time to analyze them . . .

Then let's take the time . . .

M.G.: Fine, but then Alain Badiou will have to forgive me because I might go on for a bit!

Alain Badiou: Don't worry about me, I'll be preparing for war in the meantime . . .

M.G.: The first and most important issue is to identify clearly the historical situation we're in. I think that, far from a return to the 1930s, our current situation is absolutely original. It's characterized by a striking paradox: we're witnessing the triumph of democracy, liberalism, and capitalism *and* a new and simultaneous crisis of democracy, liberalism, and capitalism. There are two sides to the picture: on the one hand, the ultimate validation of a political model (liberal democracy) and of a type of economic organization (capitalism) and, on the other, new contradictions undermining each from within.

To understand this situation, we need to go back and choose the right starting point. We automatically trace the victory of the capitalist democracies back to the fall of the Berlin Wall and the collapse of the USSR. That view strikes me as misleading. What happened in 1989, obviously without my wanting to downplay its symbolic significance, was to my mind the consequence of older and much deeper changes. After all, Communist China's conversion to a variant of capitalism preceded the fall of the Wall and can be seen to be just as important a phenomenon as the collapse of Soviet socialism. So we need to go farther back if we want to trace the genealogy of our problems.

I propose that we distinguish between two key periods of contemporary democratic history: the period 1945–75, which was a time of consolidation of democracy, and the period since 1975, which is characterized by the threefold crisis I mentioned. The period from 1945 to 1975 was the great phase of political stabilization of the Western democracies, which had emerged as the victors over fascism and Nazism. They experienced exceptional economic growth and saw a new type of capitalism develop: after the early days of extortionate capitalism, which was based on the indiscriminate exploitation of material resources and the labor force, a redistributive capitalism based on the increase in workers' purchasing power developed. It was the golden age of consumer society, when most people reaped the benefits of growth. The lasting consequence of this success was that the leaders of the social-democratic regimes developed a blind faith in the progress of capitalism. A new political mindset took hold: growth became the primary collective objective. This was the legacy of the post-war boom, the Thirty Glorious Years [*les Trente Glorieuses*], which the 1973 economic crisis did not fundamentally challenge. Even today governments seek and derive their legitimacy from their ability to achieve growth. Outside of growth there is no salvation! As for the rest, we'll see what happens afterward . . .

So in what way did the period that began in the 1970s mark a break?

M.G.: Starting in the 1970s, democracy was shaken by a major social reality: the massive individualization of societies. This phenomenon was captured in the slogan "human rights," which became the cornerstone of our regimes, the ultimate reference that made it possible to distinguish between what was legitimate in collective life and what wasn't. It's important to understand the precise meaning of this phenomenon, which corresponded to an irresistible advance of the liberal principle in our societies. People usually only see the ethical, legal, and political dimensions in human rights. But an individual does not just have rights; s/he also has interests. The novelty of the situation that began in the early 1970s stemmed from the fact that the economic aspect of individual freedoms moved to the fore and even became the privileged scope of application. The triumph of the logic of individual rights couldn't be separated from that of the principle of the maximization of these same people's interests. That's how we went from the society of rights to the market society. For, once individual actors' independence was sanctified in that way, the coordination of the whole necessarily took the shape of a market, or, in other words, of a more or less automatic trade-off between the initiatives, offers, and demands of the various actors involved. There's nothing new about these ideas per se. The novelty lies in the spread of their applications. They began to shape real social life through and through.

The democracies thus entered the age of individualism once and for all. The sentence that sums up the neoliberal age is: "There is nothing but individuals, individuals considered in isolation, who come together in competitive cooperation to ensure respect for their rights and the pursuit of their interests." This was an entirely new situation, not intellectually speaking, as I said, but practically speaking. It enables us to understand how unique our crisis is compared with that of the beginning of the twentieth century. The dominant theme of the crisis of the democracies in the early twentieth century, the one that would lead to the emergence of the totalitarian form, was the primacy of the political and its claim to organize collective life as a whole. It was inscribed in a historical context in which mass movements were constitutive. The current crisis is inscribed in a symmetrically opposite context: the disappearance of the masses, the eradication of the collective position of dominance, the unlimited demand for individual freedoms. It is the sudden emergence of the interest of the parts – individuals – against the authority of the Whole. The current categorical imperative is to free individuals as much as possible from the control of collective norms. This requires an ever-increasing juridification of economic and social relations. Previously, the law governed communities; now it has become the strong arm of triumphant individualism. This underlying axiom of life in our societies needs to be brought fully to light so that both its pervasiveness and its limits can be appreciated.

To complete this picture, you began by mentioning a crisis of capitalism that accompanied the crisis of liberal democracy. To what extent has capitalism changed in the past forty years, and what, in your opinion, are the distinguishing features of the crisis it is currently going through?

M.G.: Let me clarify something first. The concept of capitalism seems obvious to us because it's so familiar. We use the word on a daily basis. But do we really know what we're dealing with? The familiarity deceives us. The notion is by no means self-evident. Although capitalism corresponds to an undeniable empirical reality, it nonetheless requires an in-depth theoretical examination.

To begin with, we should remember that the term itself didn't originate with Marx. It was German social democracy of the late nineteenth century that sanctified it and developed a critical vulgate around it that is still referred to today, even by its most fervent proponents – which never ceases to amaze me! But we often remain at the level of a general concept of a modus operandi of collective activity focused on the economy. That's not wrong, but we need to go into greater detail. What we call "capitalism" actually combines a host of different factors. It's a "black box" containing very disparate elements: finance (capital properly speaking and the requirements for its reproduction); the structuring of transactions by the market; a recent, very special social form, the company; employees, and, last but not least, the world of sciences and technology. This list is not exhaustive. These various basic ingredients of capitalism support one another and operate together, but they must be carefully distinguished from one another. It's this "discriminating" approach that will enable us to see how much capitalism has changed in the past forty years. Everything has changed: finance has become globalized – I'll come back to this; the wage form and corporate organization have undergone profound changes; the rules in force on the markets have changed, and so on. What's more, we have entered economies of knowledge and innovation, in which science and technology are playing a crucial role in the production process.

Combine all these elements and you get a capitalism that has nothing or almost nothing to do with the capitalism whose workings Marx attempted to understand.

But what about the crisis of this new capitalism? How can it be explained?

M.G.: What's been happening since the banking and financial crisis of 2008 has brought to light a structural problem. On paper, capitalism should be in perfect health: it has never had such freedom of maneuverability. It can operate all over the world now. And yet it's ill, gravely and chronically ill. Capitalism is being eaten away from within by one its most salient aspects: economic and financial globalization. What is globalization? It's the opportunity for the most powerful players to disregard the rules defined within national spaces. A multinational can lay down the law to countries – we have clear evidence of this all the time, alas. Countries beg capital to come to them, or not to leave them ... Economic organizations have acquired an excessively wide latitude of action. This is due in large part to the financial liberalization process, which began in the late 1970s and allows sufficiently large corporate entities to expand as they see fit. As the economist Jean-Luc Gréau aptly put it, capitalism has become "sick from its own finance industry." In a matter of just 40 years or so, finance has turned into an autonomous sphere of extraction of the value produced in the real economic field. It captures and carries off the wealth produced, for the benefit of a few players. Finance is truly the Wild West in its purest form. Capitalism itself has been profoundly affected by it. During the period from 1945 to 1975 the product of economic activity was distributed through collective bargaining mechanisms, which, despite being hard to implement at times, were for the most part effective. That model, which was based on state and union mediation, was demolished. Redistributive capacity was brought to a halt and wiped out. Today, with the cancerous growth of finance, we've got a predatory capitalism, doomed to constant crisis because of its relentless headlong rush forward, driven by increasingly uncontrollable financial instruments that are out of touch with reality.

A new kind of democracy that reveres the individual, a new liberalism focused more on the individual's interests than on his/her rights and duties, a new capitalism swallowed up by finance: would these be the three aspects that you think are combined in the current crisis?

M.G.: Yes, those aspects are inextricably intertwined, but, to take my argument through to its conclusion, I'd have to say a little more, although I don't want to wear out Alain Badiou's patience . . .

A.B.: As you go along, I can sense my disagreements building up and getting stronger. So finish your remarks, and I'll hold my objections, which are, in fact, numerous and serious, in reserve.

M.G.: Thank you. That should allow us to have a real discussion about the current situation. It's worth focusing a bit on globalization, because it's the backdrop to all the changes today. The globalization that has been occurring since the 1970s is really an extraordinary transformation. Here again, let's stop and consider the very terms we use. We have this word *"mondialisation"* [literally, "worldwide-ization"] in French, which I think works fine, so let's keep it. It seems more fitting, more appropriate to me than *"globalisation,"* which is a translation of the English word "globalization." Why do I think so? Because "globalization" is limited to the sphere of economics alone. I already considered the issue of financial globalization, but it clearly goes beyond stock markets and banks today: we're living in the era of the global marketplace, quite simply. It's a situation that produces highly ambivalent effects, moreover. On the one hand, entire areas of the globe are developing economically, and we can only welcome the fact that poverty is decreasing in some regions. This positive aspect of globalization shouldn't be forgotten. We should beware of having too negative and pessimistic an interpretation – it's not hell on earth! But, on the other hand, it is true that large inequalities have been developing between countries and even within countries.

Nevertheless, economic globalization [*globalisation*] does not exhaust the phenomenon of *mondialisation*. Indeed, the latter has a much more profound, properly *political* dimension. In historical terms, in the period from 1945 to 1975, at the very time when the Western democracies were becoming stabilized, the European empires were collapsing, and the colonized nations were becoming liberated. The process changed everything dramatically all over the world. And, with the gradual development of the formerly colonized countries, we ended up with the situation we're in today, in which no power – even the American hyper-power, which has entered an obvious crisis of its dominance – can lay down the law to the world any longer. *Mondialisation* is thus defined by a general movement in which states can no longer use imperialist-type reflexes and practices. From now on they have to deal with each other in a more sophisticated way. *Mondialisation* as a political phenomenon is wholly dependent on this "de-imperializing" of the globe – as I call it – which it brings about and promotes. States no longer have the same freedom or autonomy of action, and this confronts them with new challenges.

Couldn't it be said that the key factor of the current crisis, the one that ties together the various aspects you've discussed, lies in the decline of the political itself?

M.G.: Yes, that's clear, and I'll conclude with that. With the current situation, we see the undisputed, and supposedly indisputable, primacy of economics in the trappings of globalized capitalism and a neoliberal ideology that's become absolute. This overall dynamic has been supplemented by a double elimination, or a double deconstruction, of the political. First of all, the political has been eliminated from without by the advent of globalization, which undermined the prerogatives of nation-states. Second, politics has been incapacitated from within by the unlimited assertion of individual rights, which has occurred at the expense of legitimately established collective authority. With this double deconstruction, we're right at the heart of the current crisis of the democracies, which is not a challenging of the democratic form – virtually everyone agrees in principle with that – but a crisis of the collapse of its framework, of the stripping away of its meaning. In our societies, democracy is nothing but a word now, nothing but a sham notion hiding the real, inordinate power of the individualistic model and the economic-financial complex.

If this analysis is correct, I think the crux of the change we need to imagine is the restoration of the category of the political to the center of the life of our societies. It had been hypostatized out of all proportion by the totalitarianisms that plunged the twentieth century into bloodshed. Those regimes are used as bogeymen today to justify the complete elimination of the political, or, at the very least, an attempt to gradually liquidate it. Let's forget and marginalize the political to avoid falling back into the errors of the past, we're told. This leaves the way open for the self-sufficient development of the economy. I think, on the contrary, that the political is the key to recovery. All the phenomena I've pointed out – the financialization of capitalism, the unlimited expansion of individualism – are not natural facts. They're developments with overwhelming symptoms, of course, but on which it is nonetheless possible to have an impact.

I'm convinced we're at a historical low point. We're still paralyzed by the crisis, but there are profound changes on the horizon, so great is the need for them. So I'll come back to my project, to my wager, and say that a new cycle of economic and political reforms of the democracies is within our reach. It should be at least as significant as the ones we witnessed in the early twentieth century and after 1945. With this new cycle of reforms, we'll be able to breathe vigorous new life into democracy and into the ideal of social justice that is part and parcel of it. We'll finally be in a position to control globalization and recreate the conditions of a healthier, more efficient, and more equitable economy, as it was in the past.

Now we can turn to you, Alain Badiou. What are your thoughts about this sweeping panorama that Marcel Gauchet just presented of the current situation? Do you agree with the idea of a threefold crisis combining capitalism, liberalism, and democracy, all against a backdrop of globalization? You already implied that you had some misgivings . . .

A.B.: Misgivings? You've got to be kidding! I'm in full and complete disagreement with the picture Marcel Gauchet just painted of the current situation. My disagreement is total and my opposition complete, word for word. Up to now, we could think that a rapprochement between us was generally possible, despite our opposing projects. But here, when we get to the analysis of the present, it becomes patently obvious that any lasting agreement is impossible. In what way does my diagnosis completely differ from yours? You claim that we're experiencing a totally new situation and that this situation is under the generic banner of the crisis. I maintain the exact opposite. What strikes me, on the contrary, is far more a kind of return to the past.

You ended your remarks with a reflection on globalization. I'm going to reverse your order of exposition and start with that, and then I'll get to the supposed changes in liberalism and democracy. According to you, globalization is a recent phenomenon, which came into its own after World War II. It supposedly grew at lightning speed, and today we live, to quote you, "in the era of the global marketplace." But come on! By the nineteenth century the main European economies were already largely globalized, perhaps even more so than today! At that time, the French and British empires possessed virtually all the world's wealth. Globalization is nothing but capitalism's deployment in every space available to it. Yet that – which Marx, as a matter of fact, called "the world marketplace" – is what happened in the nineteenth century and is happening again at the beginning of the twenty-first century. If there was anything really new in between them, in the twentieth century, it was only due to the emergence of the communist alternative, which blocked the natural expansion of the global marketplace for a very long time. Thus, substantial enclaves were not subject to the capitalist order. In the 1970s, capitalist globalization was very likely impeded to a large extent by the strength of the Communist bloc and the anti-colonial victories in a number of major wars of liberation. Ten years later, the USSR and the Soviet bloc collapsed, and, as a result, the primitive accumulation of capital at global level was able to start up again, as in the best days of the nineteenth century, in colossal proportions. New areas, new countries were opened up to predation, to forced development, to the exploitation of enormous masses of proletarianized peasants: China, India, and so on. Capitalism inhaled a big breath of fresh air the better to smother the newly conquered peoples and conscript them into the workings of the market. In a nutshell, there's nothing distinctive about contemporary globalization. What we are seeing is just the return to the expansion – previously blocked, now unlimited – of capital. Globalization and capitalism can't be separated; rather, they're genetically linked, and they are moving ahead together today to subjugate the whole world.

A third term has to be immediately added to this dyad: imperialism. How is it defined? Imperialism is the unassailable law and driving force of the global development of capitalism. There's no globalization without the imperial power that absorbs and concentrates capital. Thus, two modes of capital expansion were established in the nineteenth century: the rapid primitive accumulation of a number of Western centers and the colonial exploitation of resources in the rest of the world. Back then, the French and British empires divided up the world between them, economically and politically. There were of course conflicting polarities between them, but that competition was the structured form of globalization. It pitted economic operators linked to state power against one another. And what about today? The same process is at work. Globalization shouldn't be viewed as a homogeneous phenomenon. It's not! It's that same imperialist world we've returned to ever since the collapse of the USSR. Today's globalization marks the return to the normal, that is, imperial, state of capitalism. The age-old competition between imperial powers, all of them capitalist but eager to carve out a big place for themselves in the global arena, or even to acquire a hegemonic position comparable to that of the US and the dollar, is back! China and Russia are demanding their share, and many different kinds of local conflicts, causing deaths and destruction, are the rampant symptom of those rivalries. The Middle East is playing the exact same role in this as the Balkans did on the eve of World War I.

So when I hear you say with a straight face that globalization is a sign of the de-imperialization of the world, that the "empire" form is dead and buried, I'm shocked! That's a euphoric vision that's totally out of touch with observable reality. How can you maintain that there's no more imperialism when there are more and more wars, when the great powers are sending their troops into an ever-increasing number of countries? Look at the US: in competition in this regard with China, it is constantly building up, at great expense, an unprecedented military apparatus! There's no way you can make me believe it's acting that way because everything's fine among the world's peoples. Armed interventions to keep entire populations subservient are still as sad and sickening an issue today as ever. No, frankly, talking about the de-imperialization of the world is pure and simple naïveté!

If we wanted to sequence the history of modern imperialism, we could distinguish between two stages, two successive ways of acting. From the nineteenth century up to the post-World War II emancipations, imperialism was essentially inseparable from colonialism. Far-away countries were subjugated and divided up at large international conferences. During the Berlin Conference of 1884–5, the European powers carved Africa up into pieces, which they divided among themselves without consulting the indigenous peoples. This incited bitter inter-state rivalries. This first sort of imperialism came to an end with the demise of the colonial empires. But did imperialism as such disappear? No, it just took different forms, and this is what needs to be analyzed. In the past, countries were administered. Today, they're bought, piece by piece, sector by sector. This is exactly how China goes about it, and it is infiltrating old Europe: how many Greek infrastructures have become the properties of the Chinese state?

M.G.: Let me just clarify one point that's crucial for understanding our times. The historical destiny of the imperial form is a key issue. It is not just about an opinion or a political judgment: believing or not believing in the imperialist tendencies of the current powers. It has to do with a political form, empire, which has played a major role in history, from Rome to communism and colonialism, but which we have just seen collapse.

A.B.: That is in fact a crucial point, because I, for one, think there's a link that often goes unexamined not just between capitalism and imperialism but also between democracy itself and imperialism. Up to now, the only democratic societies we have known have all been in imperialistic contexts. That's been true right from the time of ancient Greece. Athenian democracy, the ancient paradigm of contemporary democracy, was only established in the context of Greek imperialism – an especially fierce imperialism. In France, the Third Republic came to power at the exact same time as the enormous expansion of the colonial empire. These associations are foundational and should be examined in depth.

M.G.: So that means we should devote a little more attention to this issue.

Chapter 6
The end of imperial logic, or the continuation?

Marcel Gauchet: Is capitalist globalization inseparable from a form of imperialism? Let's take a look at recent history. A distinction needs to be made between two eras of globalization. The first one takes us back to the late nineteenth and early twentieth centuries. Globalization at that time was inseparable from the colonial enterprise; you're right about that, Alain Badiou. The second one corresponds to the present time. But this second globalization is very different by its very nature from the earlier one. There are of course some remnants of classical imperialism. They're concentrated in that unique area of the world, Africa. In Africa today, there continues to be a form of imperialism precisely because there's an alarming political vacuum. In many countries, governments hold on in a purely spectral way; they aren't strong enough to guide the destiny of their people. This makes possible scandalous exploitation and terrible practices, perhaps even more horrifying than the worst colonial exactions of the past. In Congo, today, it's a living hell . . .

Alain Badiou: It was already like that in the past. Just think of the period of rubber production in the Congo, which was responsible for 2,000,000 deaths, unknown to Western memory. That colonization in the Congo was an eye-opening experience, but the entire colonial period was based on that model. Nowadays, the imperialist powers' policy of weakening local states, which leads to the tragic breakdown of the societies in question, is not limited to Africa, even if the complete destruction of Libya by the French and the British, ushering in decades of civil war and the exodus of entire populations, is a particularly edifying variation of it. The destruction of the Iraqi state by the US is also tragic in this respect. We have come to the bitter realization of the price that has to be paid for it.

M.G.: Yes, but at the same time we also see that that destruction was not necessarily only in the US' interest. It came with a big political price tag for its leaders. I'm certainly not going to deny the contemporary incarnations of the old imperialism. I'm not as Pollyannaish as that . . . But do we necessarily have to adopt the opposite attitude and always rehash the same old Marxisant analyses on "imperialism, the highest stage of capitalism"? It seems to me there's another aspect of globalization, one that might make us more optimistic about it. I agree that globalization is intimately bound up with capitalism and that it follows and sanctifies its logic, but that's too simplistic an explanation. You're overlooking the main aspect that I highlighted: the fact that today's globalization is also, and essentially, a political phenomenon. Today, the rise of China, of India, of Asia in general, clearly shows that there's a decentralization of economic power as compared with any imperial order whatsoever. This decentralization brings with it an element of properly political polycentrism that's completely unprecedented as compared with what we witnessed during the European states' colonial phase. In the world today there's no longer any credible candidate for global domination. Not just because no power has the means to achieve such an ambition or because other competing powers have emerged, but because the idea itself no longer makes sense. We need to appreciate the full import of this advent of a new global polycentrism! Especially since the end of imperial aspirations has in turn opened up opportunities to build societies that are more in line with the values of democracy, throughout the world.

A.B: There's your optimism again. I'm not at all sure that the emerging powers you mentioned will be amenable to a polycentric, or even "democratic," globalization, respectful of everyone's interests. China and virtually all the countries of Southeast Asia have held on to strongly authoritarian political structures. As for India, it's now being stirred up by Buddhists whose nationalistic rhetoric is particularly aggressive. In that region of the world, the general logic is still nationalistic and imperialistic. The exact same thing could be said about Putin's Russia. These new powers are taking over the stage of globalization in an often violent, aggressive way. They're demanding their share of the wealth, just as Germany, which was competing with the dominant French and British empires in the late nineteenth century, did. The result was a world war . . . You're urging us to distinguish more rigorously between two different eras of globalization. And I myself already said that we need to analyze the mutations of imperialism. Well, I'd put it like this then: the colonialism of partition was followed by the anarchy of zoning.

What is zoning? How does it differ from the imperialism of partition?

A.B.: Partition meant that they would get together to discuss parts of the world that would be assigned to such and such a power. This resulted in mapped-out divisions as the consequence of international conferences. It's not done like that anymore. This change can be explained by the liberations of the past, by the fact that inter-imperialist rivalries had to contend with the struggles for national liberation (the old empires were no longer as powerful). Within the newly won freedom of the formerly colonized countries zoning was practiced. Zoning is a set of practices that involve pre-empting strategic economic enclaves for their mining, timber, agricultural, etc. resources. The new-style imperial powers reserve oil, mining, etc. zones for themselves and occupy them. They acquire the monopoly on exploitation of the local resources. They take advantage of the extreme state of decline of the countries concerned – in Africa today, entire regions are characterized by purely sham states – and do all they can to exacerbate this devastated state of affairs. When a state is in a position to claim its own share, they speed up its destruction by financing armed rebels, for example, who do the dirty work needed to destabilize it. In the end, the systematic looting of resources, which involves creating safe enclaves, leads to an even more devious and murderous imperialism and to rampant lawlessness that plunges entire countries into chaos. When you see how all the great powers scramble and struggle to "zone," to use exclusive contractual agreements to set up miniature states within established states – look at Areva in Niger; it's a French state within the Niger state – how can you, once again, talk about a de-imperialization of the world? Wherever there's money to be made, borders become blurry, heavily armed (by whom?) groups roam the countryside, and forces, whether Western or other, secure the profitable zones under various "humanitarian" pretexts. This zoning is not exclusive to the US and Europe; everyone is in on it! This is the terrifying face of globalization today. In the past, you could see all the imperial powers meeting, as they did in Berlin in 1884–5, to divvy up among themselves the world's remaining parcels of land with high economic potential. If they wanted peace, there would be peace. But if the US (which thinks of itself as the only genuine state at world level), China, Russia, and so on, feel they've been wronged in the international community and want to wage war, what will happen? The UN, as everyone can see, is a conveyor belt for Western interests in zoning. Elsewhere, national sentiments are still strong enough for the emerging great powers, whose capitalist development, whether "democratic" or not, is rapid, to arm their citizens and have them launch an attack. I don't believe in the long life of so-called "peace" today. If a communist-type hypothesis isn't imposed at global level, as a force for peace, the history of the current century will prove the truth of the statement both Jaurès and Lenin made: "Imperialism [whether zoning or colonies] carries war within it the way storm clouds carry the storm." Let's not forget that the wars after 1945, in which the imperial powers were regularly involved, caused many more deaths than World War II itself.

There are two common ways of fetishizing globalization: it's considered either as a post-state era or as an ordinary period in history characterized by a withering away of national sentiment. These two aspects obviously come together in the diagnosis of the end or the "crisis" of the nation-state form. But come on, let's open our eyes, let's "globalize" our vision! The most powerful states are certainly not the puppets or the dupes of globalization. There's nothing to support the idea that they've melted into a sort of great global homogenization of decision-making actors. The US remains the systemic center of world capitalism, and it clings tenaciously to that status. If that's not tangible proof of its greedy lust for power, then I don't know what is . . . As for the decline of the feeling of belonging to a nation, that's a European and solely European symptom. Your conception of a polycentric globalization is based on the idea that states will weaken to the point where they'll go along of their own accord with the political consensus, and national passions will merge into the global consensus around capitalism and democracy. That kind of globalization is an illusion as compared with real globalization. Outside of Europe the dynamic is not moving at all in the direction you mentioned. I'm struggling to shake off a nagging feeling. You often refer to "our societies." But what exactly are you talking about? What's your vantage point? Isn't it anything but global? Aren't you thinking exclusively from the standpoint of "our" declining European model? Your analytical approach strikes me as fixated on, obsessed by, Europe. I'm sorry, but that's tunnel vision . . .

M.G.: You're right, that's an important point that needs to be clarified. The geographical and geopolitical focus of my analyses is in fact Europe. "Our societies," mine and yours, are the European and American capitalist democracies, or, in other words, the so-called "West." I pay particular attention to Europe because it's there that the modern project first developed, and its trajectory still has exemplary value, the equivalent of which the US, despite its power and dynamism, doesn't provide. The US is a special case, in fact, on the basis of the same principles. Now, I don't hold the Old Continent sacred. Like you, I think it is plunged in utter confusion. This needs to be accounted for by going beyond the sole diagnosis of a collapse of nation-states. The state of decline is linked precisely to globalization, which signals a "de-Europeanization" and a "de-Westernization" of global history. Europe no longer has the monopoly on, or the intellectual leadership of, modernity, as it had for so long, even in the midst of American dominance. More to the point, globalization – and in this respect it really does bring a new phenomenon with it – coincides with the independent appropriation by extra-Western political communities of the instruments of modernity developed in the West. Europe is being challenged on its own turf, in its native specificity. It now has to deal at global level with actors that have taken over ways of thinking and operating that originated with it. That explains its current unease. It is having a hell of a time contending with the loss of its intellectual and political influence, even though, in a way, it "inspires" the whole world. This is the paradox that unsettles and character-izes it. Elsewhere, the issues are different. We mentioned Africa, but its own challenges are totally different.

Our world is not uniform or synchronous. As soon as you talk about globalization, you're dealing with differential geography. That's the principle of a genuine political thinking of globalization. It doesn't mean the eradication of the nation-state form. On the contrary, I agree with you, states are still extremely powerful actors today. And it's not necessarily a question of size, to refute a false argument that's often invoked. Take Singapore: here's a "little" state, from the geographical point of view, which nevertheless reports remarkable economic numbers and has a lot of political influence in the Southeast Asian region. No, the novelty is that nation-states today are structures opening onto a global horizon. No state, even the richest, the most powerful, or the most developed one, can any longer act as the center of a sphere to which it dictates. It has to reckon with partners near and far, which are in a way on an equal footing with it.

A.B.: Once again, what's so new about that? In the nineteenth century, imperial England was already connected to a global horizon. Matters concerning India or Australia were addressed in London. The British community was even more globalized than in the twentieth century! The global marketplace is simply more complex today.

M.G.: Nineteenth-century England was a colonial power, and it no longer is – that's the whole difference. The scale of what we regard as "global" has become incomparable, so there's been a change in kind, not just in degree. Today's globalization poses a problem that was never so great in scope or importance before: the problem of the connection between the nation-state level and the global level. The nation-state is still the properly political standard, because it's within its framework that citizens participate in democratic life – if we're in a democracy. If we move onto the global level, the question of internationalism, of the concertation among state actors, arises. So far, however, economics has reigned supreme in this sphere. We haven't yet managed to achieve a properly political, sufficiently democratic linkage between the two levels. That is the present challenge.

A.B.: You're disregarding Europe, for once. What has the construction of Europe been if not an attempt to connect established nation-states and a newly established higher order?

M.G.: In principle, yes, Europe was the blueprint for a project of that sort, but in reality it has turned out to be a terrible missed opportunity. The European Community was the result of naïve internationalism. In context, the idea of a unification of war-torn, barely reconciled nation-states was perfectly understandable. "Rising above national interests" was a good slogan for defusing potential emotionally charged conflicts. But Europe ultimately created a monster that is satisfactory neither in terms of nation-states nor in terms of the inscription in a global horizon. It's this last issue that needs to be addressed: the real, reasonable opening up to globalization. The challenge is to create a genuine democratic space within the Union and to define relationships with the rest of the world that are regulated by the political.

A.B.: As things stand now, the sovereign commissions that are presiding over the fate of the European Union are agents of sovereign neoliberalism. The political won't prevail so easily.

M.G.: Sure, but those institutions are neither effective nor democratic, and that's where the failure comes from!

A.B.: That's not failure, it's success! One of the distinguishing features of the construction of Europe is to impose measures and reforms on states in line with the demands of the financial oligarchy. In actual fact, the commissions are playing an accelerating, indisputably mediating role between capitalist globalization and the European nation-states, weakening the latter on behalf of the big capitalist groups' interests. We can't and won't be able to count on Europe to resist the orders of Google et al.

M. G.: But why not? This is where a strong political will is indispensable. I'm aware of how hard it is to move toward what I'm proposing, but it doesn't seem purely utopian to me.

A.B.: On the European issue as on the others, you act as if there were good intentions in politics, provided it's "democratic" in the way you mean it. I may seem overly gloomy or pessimistic to you, but no, we shouldn't act as if there were good intentions in "democratic" politics. There's only business and interests, and also, with the rejection of any general idea of emancipation, a cowardly and fearful consensus in a very large proportion of public opinion aimed at preserving Western privileges indefinitely. As a result of this there is a despicable and increasingly patent flirtation with cultural racialism, the notion of the West's superiority, and, more broadly speaking, the fear of foreigners, of immigrants, who supposedly take food from our table. The politicians of the "democracies" at the service of capital are constantly "excusing" these aberrations on the basis of "the difficulties of the situation." To regain our dignity and good sense, we must break completely with the idea that our political system can have good intentions.

M.G.: But it can! It has happened in the past, if I'm not mistaken. Why rule out such a possibility in that way? Basically, that's the source of our disagreement. It concerns the general tone of our remarks, and I, for my part, acknowledge my optimistic side.

A.B.: I'm trying to look at the situation as a whole, and I see that, throughout my political life, those who have governed us, the countries of Europe, and France in particular, were anything but angels.

M.G.: Since the 1980s perhaps, but that was the precise time when the neoliberalism we're both fighting became dominant. The lack of good intentions is not an ontological property of politicians. You wouldn't say it is, surely.

A.B.: No, I wouldn't go that far. Evil is not lodged for all eternity in those who are called to power. But Europe today is led by people who handle it like a constraint operator: Europe requires such and such a deficit reduction, Europe requires such and such a policy with devastating social effects. And, when the citizens are asked to express their opinion about the European Union, we know what a rejection that can lead to. The corollary of globalization is the relentless determination to minimize states, to sidestep or forcibly subordinate the local level to global requisites, whose substance we've described. So Europe doesn't carry much weight in the face of globalization? That's because it has become its accomplice.

M.G.: And that's what has to be changed.

Alain Badiou, one clarification before we perhaps end this substantive exchange on globalization. At what level do you situate the possible and necessary development of the communist hypothesis? Where do you think we have to start from to free ourselves from capitalism? What is the relevant space of reflection and action?

A.B.: I already touched on this when I was defining communism. On this issue my position is the classic Marxist one: the real level of political construction is global. Of course, the communist hypothesis must be verified through local popular movements. But as for its overall vision, its space of experimentation, of failure or success, it encompasses and concerns the world as a whole. When you have an adversary, you need to try to measure up to it, and capitalism is a global force . . . In historical communism, internationalism was a fiction for the most part. The USSR and China, sometimes despite their rhetoric, held to a narrow national logic – ideologically, not geographically narrow! Turning inward is a dead end, we now know that it ultimately serves what we want to combat. The isolationist or protectionist flag, waved right here in France by the far left, a part of the left, and the whole far right, gets us nowhere. Suppose a state decides to withdraw from the international consensus: it will almost immediately be subjected to ostracism, to a boycott such that the cost of the initiative will be devastating within a very short time. No one can really believe in the soundness and effectiveness of a project like that. No one wants to create a little, isolated France, entrenched behind its borders, which would become impoverished in record time. Only the far right relishes this identitarian fantasy that would drive us into powerlessness. So the communist hypothesis must prove itself locally while at the same time taking over the world stage. And that enlightened internationalism will be the impetus for a combination of initiatives that will combat today's capitalist globalization, which isolates and enslaves at every level.

Chapter 7
The deconstruction of capitalism

After dealing in detail with the question of globalization, we can now move on to the other two major issues that Marcel Gauchet raised in his overview of the contemporary world: the crisis of capitalism, which has become "sick from its own finance industry," and the crisis of democracy, stripped of its ability to self-govern politically by the new neoliberal spirit that reduces everything to a matter of individual rights and interests. Alain Badiou, do you think we've entered a neoliberal era that's paralyzing the democracies? And, in your opinion, is the current crisis of capitalism related to the autonomy of the financial sphere?

Alain Badiou: Yes, the discussion we had about globalization shouldn't make us forget everything else! Especially since I also disagree completely about these other two issues . . . I was really surprised when Marcel Gauchet spoke about an unprecedented advance of the liberal principle in our societies, in both the economic sphere and the political field. According to him, there's been a profound ideological transformation going on for the past 40 years. Capitalism and democracy, he says, have become sick from the priority accorded individuals and their interests. That's a strange view . . . Liberalism – the doctrine that there are only individuals – has from the start been nothing less than the very theoretical basis of the thinkers of capitalism. Capitalism inherently needs an anthropological conception of that sort. Nothing is more important to it than this vision of sovereign individuals living together harmoniously thanks to the miraculous intervention of the invisible hand . . . It is capitalism itself that leads us into the era of individuals, and that's not a recent phenomenon. The current system isn't in crisis; on the contrary, it's in perfect health! The way you see it, democracy is succumbing to the liberal virus. The way I see it, the link between parliamentary democracy and liberalism is anything but a historical contingency. Is democracy today corrupted by the effects of interindividual free competition? No, that's its very essence. You know, when you believe that the only acceptable political decision is one made in an isolated voting booth [*isoloir*] – the word is particularly apt and revealing – you can't then complain about the fact that people reason from a strictly personal point of view.

In essence, capitalism brings liberalism and democracy together. It is nothing but the possibility of merging, of blurring the difference between, *homo oeconomicus* and *homo politicus*. The subject who is called upon to vote is exactly the same as the subject who appears before the market. There is only one type of individual, economic because s/he aims to satisfy his/her interests, and political because s/he's considered to be the basic unit of decision-making. I have the impression that you'd like to separate the two aspects, to subtract *homo oeconomicus* from *homo politicus*. But that's impossible, because they're two sides of the same coin. It always comes back to what I call the big Other of the democratic scene: capital, which ideologically and politically controls parliamentary democracy – which is therefore not in "crisis" but in a situation that's completely normal for it. Liberal democracy is logically based on the consumer-purchaser as the anthropological figure of existing society. Therefore, what you denounce as a perversion of democracy is actually only the resounding confirmation of its true nature.

Still, Alain Badiou, is there really nothing new under the sun? Would you go so far as to deny that capitalism today is in crisis?

A.B.: Fine, let's talk about the economic crisis. Is it really a new phenomenon? Well, no, there was nothing new about the crisis that began in 2008 either! It was an ordinary crisis of over-production, as we've experienced in the past. To attribute it, as you do, Marcel Gauchet, to a fatal splitting off of finance is absurd. What actually happened? The whole subprimes business was a completely classic trigger: in the US, they wanted to sell houses en masse to people who borrowed the money to buy them and ultimately couldn't pay it back. The financial industry only got involved because it wanted to sell that debt all over the world. That's what's always been done! They've always wanted to sell debt all over the world. As my friend the economist Pierre-Noël Giraud puts it, capitalism is essentially a "business of promises." Already in the sixteenth century, when some merchant invested in a ship to sail to far-off islands, he was sold the promise that it wouldn't sink, via a system of insurance ... And even if a catastrophe occurred he wouldn't lose too much. In the imperial Europe of the nineteenth century, the financial sphere was already well established and very powerful. There were a lot more people living off income from property than there are today. Income investment, after all, is the milking of the productive sphere by the financial sphere. There was never any separation between the two spheres, any more then than now – that's a myth. Financialization is the very essence of capitalism, because capitalism is necessarily anticipatory profit. To anticipate is to take a risk, and finance exists to sell that risk on a market. It takes the form of a system of credits, of various securities that are bought and exchanged. Obviously, the more the market expands, the more the risks increase. Control over the actors who rush the promises into circulation decreases. In 2008, people were promised that they'd be able to meet their commitment, but they weren't able to. The banks were in dire straits because they'd chopped up the debt into pieces to sell it, because they'd excessively "securitized" (that's what it's called) it. And the system then collapsed like a house of cards. Governments were called to the rescue, and they came, because they had a vital need to maintain the logic of primitive capital accumulation.

In the end, the 2008 crisis seems like a serious crisis to me, of course, but a localized and fixable one. It was by no means the "final" crisis of capitalism, as is trumpeted here and there. I note moreover that it has created less global turmoil than the crisis of 1929. And, in the near future, you'll see that it will actually have made it possible to re-use the same mechanisms that were sneered at by those who are disdainful of finance and want to "reform" it. Capital concentration will resume with a vengeance, and it will emerge even more dominant. By virtue of their very recurrence, crises are part of the true nature of capital: Marx understood this very well, and this thesis has been confirmed once again.

So I've dealt with the current situation as I see it from three different viewpoints: the geostrategic (with globalization), the ideological (with liberalism), and the economic (with capitalism). We have a better sense now of the huge gulf between us.

Marcel Gauchet: Yes, I give you credit for formulating a completely different diagnosis from mine! As regards the current situation, a theoretical choice has to be made. Are we witnessing a return to the normal operation of capitalism and globalization, after a century-long parenthesis that would extend, let's say, from 1880 to 1980? Or are we instead dealing with a sort of great leap forward . . .

A.B.: Right, let's speak Chinese . . . (*Laughter.*)

M.G.: . . . a great leap forward that's confronting us with an unprecedented economic, political, and geostrategic situation? That's what I, for one, tend to think. Of course, as regards the general description, we may be in agreement – and many aspects do argue in favor of what you pointed out. Nevertheless, I stand by everything I said: I firmly believe that we're justified in speaking of an ongoing de-imperialization of the world and of a veritable *neo*liberalism. It's essential to highlight these differences between us, because they take us back to the hypotheses that each of is defending.

A.B.: Exactly, that's a very interesting point of methodology. It's always hypotheses that inform analyses, not the other way around. That's a general rule we're proving brilliantly at this stage of the conversation. As we don't have the same hypothesis, we don't make the same analysis. As a result, it's easier to perceive our disagreement in the analysis. When you say that you'd like to see a democracy capable of muzzling the economic powers, I can't disagree completely. But when we return to the analysis informed by a completely different hypothesis, well, there, our difference of opinion is glaringly obvious. As regards a situation that appears symptomally as a situation of crisis, there's always an initial response that amounts to saying: "There really *is* a crisis," and that's your perspective.

M.G.: Absolutely.

A.B.: And your position gives this crisis a much wider and more innovative significance than it's usually given. I say that very sincerely. You go beyond the economic crisis alone and extend the situation to the political form of democracy. You believe in its potential resurrection, because you identify factors that you think undermine it only contingently. But, as I see it, what you call "the crisis of democracy" is just its basic crushing by capitalism, its total and original dependence on that enormous historico-economic pillar. This is the other approach: the crisis can then be said to be one in appearance only, to be just a confirmation of the supposedly shaky system. If that's the diagnosis that's made, it's because a completely different hypothesis is being defended: the hypothesis that it's possible to exit that system completely – I'll let you guess what hypothesis I'm talking about . . .

M.G.: Wait, let me think . . . (*Laughter.*) The methodological point is very clear: follow the analysis and you'll get the hypothesis. Clearly, we're back at the frontlines of our battle. You pit communism against capitalism, while I want to rethink the connection between democracy and capitalism. But actually, if each of us tried to view capitalism a little more concretely . . .

A.B.: Concretely? What do you mean?

M.G.: I have the feeling that you view it monolithically. A little while ago I said that capitalism, what we commonly call "capitalism," actually refers to a variety of convergent but heterogeneous elements. Conversely, both proponents and critics, both those pro and those con, regard it as one homogeneous bloc. They make it into an entity with a mind of its own. They attribute an internal coherence to capitalism that it actually doesn't have. This concept, whose seeming unity is an illusion, needs to be deconstructed. To speak of a system or a general logic of capitalism is to view it as a whole, from above. If that point of view is adopted, the only conceivable, reasonable project is to abolish it, or at least to rise to its level it by dominating it with an even stronger political structure. This necessarily leads to increasingly authoritarian forms of organization of collective life, and we saw what that meant in the USSR . . .

My perspective requires a drastic change in the way we look at it. We need to tackle the problem the other way around and not view capitalism from above but from below, by identifying its basic elements. Let's strip capitalism to its bare bones. Let's take it apart. We need to put the motor on the table and see how it's made. If we attempt a serial analysis of capitalism, then we'll be able to act on the factors we've isolated beforehand one by one. The view of the economy as being completely subject to political dictates would no longer be appropriate. By contrast, it would seem to be possible to control capitalism by improving our detailed understanding of it and by regulating some of its basic aspects that appear to be problematic.

Let's take an example. If we analyze capitalism from below, as I encourage us to do, we're quickly led back to the basic economic unit: the business. As with capitalism, the term seems to be self-evident. But do we really know what a business is? I'm surprised to note that we don't have a clear and relevant definition of it.

How are businesses conceived of in today's capitalism? As corporations, period! You don't have to be a rocket scientist to see that a business can't be reduced to that one dimension. To be satisfied with that is to reinforce and perpetuate capital's power over those who produce it in the first place. Yet a business can and should also be defined by its purpose, its history, the composition of its employees, the things it produces or the services it renders, and so on. It is absolutely necessary to give serious consideration to this question of its definition and its legal status. If there's a communist world someday, it will be made up of businesses too!

A.B.: I'm not so sure about that . . . The business is certainly not the unsurpassable, definitive unit of everyday economic organization. There have been attempts to do without that model, in Maoist China in particular. They converted some factories there into real communal-life centers: the workers' lives, the education and healthcare systems, even a part of agricultural activity were all connected and integrated into the production effort, in a single place. That experiment turned out to be unsatisfactory, largely for political reasons, but those factories were not strictly speaking businesses. They became new forms of collective life.

M.G.: To me, that example seems more in line with a total hegemony of the business model over collective life, with a very strong basis in tradition moreover.

A.B.: I used it to show that something else is conceivable. Unlike businesses, the Chinese factories weren't for sale. And the people who worked in them could coordinate different aspects of their lives as workers, including housing, cultural, educational, and health-related aspects, which were usually unobtainable in factory-businesses.

M.G.: In this case, the factories weren't for sale, but they belonged to the Party, which appointed their managers.

A.B.: That's another story.

M.G.: It's important nonetheless . . .

A.B.: My point is that the word "business" belongs to the standard capitalist lexicon. Just listen to its apologists – that's all they ever talk about! Beware of that term, which is part of the most basic liberal propaganda. How many times have we been told about "the entrepreneurial spirit," the "entrepreneurial" genius! The business is the purest fetish of liberalism!

Ultimately, a business is always an organization whose founder, preferably someone young and brash, can be identified and which can be sold on the market at any time for a fabulous price. The term "start-up" is even preferable, to sound dynamic and like an English speaker. The dominance of private capital and the law of its circulation seem to me to be part and parcel of the notion of a business. Unless it's possible to nationalize it, a business is defined by the simple fact that it can be bought.

M.G.: Not necessarily! That's how things happen, but it's not a natural fact. We're not bound for all eternity to this conception. The status of businesses, which includes the conditions of their transferability on the market, is a convention we can both reflect and act on. A profoundly different conception from the one prevailing in our technico-commercial world is conceivable. And maybe someday we'll even be able to do without the term "business." The argument you're trying to start strikes me as being essentially over semantics. But what I'm interested in is the joint approach we should take. My ambition is to fight and beat the neoliberals on their own turf. I'm going to propose another example, as the previous one wasn't very successful . . . Nowadays, the kind of accounting we use doesn't include labor as an asset but as an expense. To work for a business isn't to bring one's skills to it but to be an expense for it. This is a strange and rather shocking view ... Labor may very well be regarded as an asset!

A.B.: There will always be people who say that labor is an expense before it's an investment, and that that expense should be reduced. This notion underlies the current incessant wave of relocations, which is spreading virtually everywhere.

M.G.: Of course. What I want to emphasize is that the rules in force in today's capitalism should be examined methodically. And, if we have clear ideas and the necessary political will, they can be changed.

A.B.: Your piece-by-piece deconstruction is a largely utopian exercise in tightrope-walking. The dismantling of capitalism will always be met with such fierce resistance that the cause will forever be lost in advance.

M.G.: We'll see about that ...

A.B.: Oh, yes, we'll see all right that the capitalists won't let themselves be dismantled so easily! Your analysis proceeds by breaking things down until the smallest factors of capitalism are clarified. However, and this is the dimension you overlook, there is a fundamental interrelationship between these basic components. You can't act on one or the other of them without unraveling what ties them inextricably together. This primordial knot, which knits and weaves the whole together, is none other than private property. We always come back to this perennial problem, which, in the final analysis, is the very crux of the debate. Private property is the untouchable dogma, the sacred cow of capitalism. Without directly challenging private property you'll never be able to undermine the system you condemn. And don't tell me I'm just recycling an outmoded idea. The key word of our times is really "privatization." On the local level, it's the very form taken by globalization. Education, healthcare, entire swaths of public services, and even essential functions of the state are overwhelmingly privatized today, in countless numbers of countries. Even the armies are privatized, in Iraq, for example, where the US directly finances mercenary groups. Capital's appropriation of collective organizations, of sectors traditionally vested in state authority, is crushing our societies like a steamroller.

M.G.: That's true, and, in fact, private property *is* a central issue. I'm not a private property fanatic, and I'm not going to launch into a resounding plea in defense of it. I personally don't regard private property as the sacred cow of the religion of freedom.

A.B.: I wasn't accusing you of that. It's regarded as such by liberals.

M.G.: Thanks, that's reassuring! When you defined what you mean by the communist hypothesis, you began with the demand for deprivatization of the global productive process.

A.B.: Yes, I've definitely got it in for private property.

M.G.: As a way out of it, you continue to call for the collective appropriation of the means of production, a notion that's basically quite obscure, even in Marx himself.

A.B.: That's no doubt true: he was pretty evasive about the issue. Nevertheless, Marx never conceived of collective appropriation in terms of exclusive state ownership of the means of production. Furthermore, within the communist constellation, which included a number of anarchists and Fourierists, the issue of collective ownership was examined closely. It wasn't a watchword that remained on a purely theoretical level.

M.G.: I take your point. But still, communist thought in the broadest sense of the term became locked in a titanic struggle – either private property or collective ownership – that severely limited its possibilities. The issue of a potential middle term was never really raised. Collective ownership remained the regulative horizon of communism as an idea. But if we turn to the experience of historical communism, what have we learned? That the program of the collective appropriation of the means of production, when put into practice, can be a trap with toxic effects, the most notable of these being that replacing shareholders with managers doesn't make for much of an improvement. If it is held to be a guiding principle not just in theory but for practice as well, collective ownership inevitably leads to a dead end. One of the chief lessons of actually existing socialism was that it is extremely difficult to devise a reasoned and reasonable, democratic and effective way of managing collective ownership. We don't have the political resources to implement it satisfactorily. Let's face it, in economic terms the Communist bloc's centralized system was an out-and-out failure. And nothing ever came of the promise of democracy that collective ownership held out. I'm judging this impossible hypothesis and this insurmountable challenge on the basis of history. We need to abandon the dogma of private property but without clinging unilaterally to its opposite, collective ownership, which is not a viable alternative.

A.B.: So you reject the collective appropriation of the means of production as an irremediably obsolete hypothesis. In your own way, you accept that things are set in stone, and I'm going to tell you why I think they're not.

As regards the private property/collective ownership opposition, the first thing to note is that this tension runs through the whole history of the modes of production, to use Marx's term. Well before the development of the communist idea as such, the formation of groups of wealthy owners, their control over political power, and the problematic nature of such domination were always issues. There were slave owners, landlords, and, with the coming of capitalism, business owners. Revolts against the order thus established always occurred, and alternative approaches were always developed. The intention was to put an end to an economic and social organization, private property, the protest against which wasn't exclusively the preserve of the communist idea. Second, you refer to the historical experience of the socialist states. The lesson I've learned from that experience when it comes to this issue is not that collective ownership is essentially doomed to failure and inefficiency. What I note above all is that, in the USSR and elsewhere, the collective appropriation of the means of production was systematically interpreted as the establishment of state ownership. Collective and state ownership were merged and conflated. This resulted in a greatly over-extended and dogmatic program of nationalizations. State ownership is a figure of the potential perversion of collective ownership, not its essential principle. It is even ultimately complicit with what the regime wants to do away with. Collectivizations and nationalizations can very well be the corollaries of a firmly established state capitalism, as the about-turn taken by China (officially communist politically, fiercely capitalist economically) has shown.

Today, to destroy the enemy's power, to put an end to private property and a close-knit oligarchy's monopoly on capital and the means of production, nationalization is not in itself the right option if the means of action and the right of control of all the actors in the nationalized site are not specified. What's more, the pure state-based strategy is obsolete in the context of globalized economies. Adhering to it is ultimately tantamount to a narrow, crassly nationalistic perspective. We need to invent different kinds of collective appropriation and define types of management that are truly democratic at every conceivable level. Instead of doing things in a static way, through over-generalization – and moving monolithically and violently from private property to state ownership, as was done up to then – we need to attempt local, progressive, multi-layered experiments.

The principle is clear enough, but what might these non-state-controlled forms of collective ownership be like in practice? Without asking you to write a political program or draft a constitution, do you have any concrete models in mind?

A.B.: I'm sure you understand that an immediate and detailed program of that sort can hardly be requested. The objective is to get out of a centuries-old situation, and that can't be done with a snap of the fingers. When it comes to this issue, we're forced to proceed by trial and error, and it's hardly surprising that the first conceivable approaches should be simplistic and misguided. I'd say that the approaches need to be multifaceted. There's no one single solution or magic bullet. A local grocery store doesn't need to be state-owned. It can belong to the people in the neighborhood, who will run it and collectively define the conditions of redistribution of the business's profits. An enterprise that centralizes the agricultural resources of a region can be controlled directly by the local residents and producers. In both these cases, care must be taken to ensure that the political bodies dealing with these enterprises aren't owners themselves, or else a new conservative bureaucratic class will be created. I'm sketching out – very roughly, I admit – some possible scenarios here, which can moreover fit in with the old model of cooperation. But it's certainly not up to us philosophers to dictate the new forms of economic organization. The actors involved on the local, regional, etc. levels must create and run them themselves. It's their decision and their responsibility, in the subjectively accepted framework of a communist strategy. A bit like what was done in the 1970s by the Lip factory workers, who developed original approaches to self-management. The field of experimentation must remain open. And, ideally, the state itself should accept or even promote these kinds of approaches, even if they challenge its own reproduction. As for me, I'm attentive to the emergence of the new, I'm always on the lookout for an event. Montaigne famously said: "When I dance, I dance; when I sleep, I sleep." Well, when I militate, I militate! I don't reach out to factory workers, to immigrant workers, with preconceived ideas and manuals for practical action in my pocket. I listen to what they say and I observe what's being invented. The communist hypothesis is connected to the local innovations aimed at undermining, from within or without, the primacy of private property. How does the reformist hypothesis tackle the problem?

M.G.: By introducing a slight difference. To my mind, private property isn't *the* problem. The real issue is the *rights* acquired through private ownership of an asset or capital. Today, I completely agree with you about this: the principle has been hypostatized and given carte blanche. As a result of which, you only have to own 15 percent of a company's capital to announce a layoff plan and leave hundreds or even thousands of employees jobless. How can anyone accept this sort of social barbarism that legitimates itself on the basis of the most perverse neoliberal ideology? I, for one, can't. There is no compelling reason for rights acquired through private property ownership to allow such practices. We can imagine a structural reform of the legal framework that would restrict private property, in a way that's far more respectful of individuals and the collective interest.

I'd like to go back to a word you used: "experimentation." That word is key. I firmly believe in the need for political and social imagination. In the past, it led to remarkable progress and valuable lessons – the self-management movement, to use your example, produced some initiatives that were anything but foolish.

Nowadays, we're faced with a shortage of creativity. Imagination is on the decline, and the prevailing intellectual desert fuels the current feeling of deadlock.

A.B.: If what's meant by reformism is the need for experimentation in politics, I can only agree. That's a broad enough definition for me to be considered a respectable reformist . . .

M.G.: You ought to thank me! Actually, just as an aside, I understand your irony regarding reformism. In the second half of the nineteenth century and again in the early twentieth century, the political debate was organized around a powerful alternative: that between reform and revolution. Today, the dilemma makes us smile, because the big choice has faded away. Real reformism is dead, just like the idea of revolution moreover! We don't know what it refers to anymore, we have to go back to our history books.

A.B.: Yes, you have to beware when you hear politicians today use the word "reform" . . .

M.G.: It's usually just trivialities or nonsense! In practice, reformism is reflected in a "lite" redistributionism – they'll lower some tax to boost some business sector, they'll tinker minimally with income tax rates or wages to placate some localized social discontent. If someone's unlucky enough to try to push redistributionism too far, s/he'll be put in his/her place because, they say, it would hamper overall effectiveness. Any serious attempt at reformism is inevitably put on the defensive and condemned as unrealistic, or irresponsible. The social democrats seem to have no other vision than to try to preserve the minimal number of economic and social gains from earlier periods that are now being threatened.

A.B.: The social democrats can't even hold on to the gains you mention. The achievements of the successive reformist waves of the twentieth century are in the process of being dismantled.

M.G.: Yes, that is in fact the current trend, and through some amazing verbal hocus-pocus what we now call "structural reforms" actually consist in undoing what the "structural reforms" of the early twentieth century and the post-World War II period had introduced. In the past, labor rights were regulated, wage conditions were protected, nationalizations took place, and the mechanisms of the welfare state were established. Now, labor rights are being relaxed, employees' job security is being threatened, and things are being privatized and denationalized. Official reformism has become a sham. It's now the enforcer, and a respectable one, of neoliberalism. We have a choice between out-and-out greed and greed with a few scruples and marginal adjustments.

A.B.: I couldn't have said it better myself . . .

M.G.: Yes, but here's the thing: reformism can and must be reformed. And I think new experiments are possible within the democratic framework we're familiar with. As regards the capitalist setup, this involves tackling three problems head-on. What are the units we think are the basis of economic activity and how should their legal status be conceived? This is the issue of businesses that was already mentioned. Second, what are the levels of economic organization? And finally, what is the appropriate, desirable mode of coordination of these units and levels? Up to now, we've failed to deal correctly with this third fundamental problem. I don't envisage any more than you do a centralized mode of coordination, in which the state would dictate and decide on everything from above. The opposite logic that calls for coordinating everything from below – this is the approach of generalized local self-management, for example – seems unworkable to me in practice. So an intermediate solution needs to be found to ensure a free linkage between the different actors and levels. Classically, that's called the market. The market is seemingly very simple: there's a meeting between supply and demand, a price is set, trade develops, and so on. But the problem, as we see all the time, is that the market is not a panacea. If we show some imagination, we might very well conceive of and implement a completely different mode of coordination. We surely don't need the communist hypothesis to do so or to force the paragons of today's capitalism into submission. Your hypothesis can only work within the framework you want to withdraw from. And since you seem to rule out the authoritarian seizure of power . . .

A.B.: I don't rule out the non-authoritarian seizure of power . . .

M.G.: That's precisely what's called democracy! It's only within that framework that real innovations can occur, and that's why it's so modern.

Alain Badiou, Marcel Gauchet has attempted to analyze what a politics of capitalism, attentive to its basic components and its contemporary transformations, might be. Is communism as you defend it simply the revival of an old idea or are you concerned with adapting it to modernity?

A.B.: That question is of the utmost importance. Marcel Gauchet, you inscribed your defense of liberal democracy in the broader notion of modernity as the emergence of autonomy. That made me think. It prompted me to situate my notion of communism historically. So I in turn would like to try to inscribe my hypothesis in what I perceive to be the becoming of modernity. To formalize the current situation at world level, I propose to draw a diagram. I enjoy thinking like a mathematician, as you know . . .

M.G.: There's nothing like math, in effect, to bring communism up to date . . . But tell me, what type of mathematics are you going to use? Algebra or geometry?

A.B.: As a good Platonist, geometry obviously . . . No, seriously now, I propose a square diagram, composed of two perpendicular axes, with each axis extending between two poles [see appendix, p. 150]. The first axis, which is vertical, represents a general opposition between tradition and modernity. The second axis, which is horizontal, corresponds to the conflictual polarity between communism – or socialism, or anti-capitalism, if you want to use an even broader notion – and capitalism. Tradition/modernity, capitalism/anti-capitalism: those are our two directional lines and our four major poles.

The world, in all its regions, is caught in this first conflict between tradition and modernity, which is revealed through a host of disparate but convergent phenomena: the resurgence of the far right in Europe, the extremist fringes, such as the Tea Party in the US, a part of the Palestinian situation, Islamist terrorism, rampant Buddhism in India, the paranoid or even psychotic self-isolation of North Korea, where every reference to communism has been deleted from the constitution in favor of an ultra-nationalistic model, and so on. All the movements and ideologies that operate in an identitarian framework, that mobilize reactive categories of a national, linguistic, or cultural nature, signify this persistence of tradition even within modernity held up as a bogeyman. In parliamentary democracies like our own, the right/left opposition is part of this split: the right's obsession is to maintain traditional features in collective life, while the left emphasizes modernity.

The basic problem is that capitalism, with its so to speak ambiguous disposition, can be connected to modernity as well as to tradition. It wants to be the law of the world, and its hegemonic pretension prevents it from being only either a rearguard or a vanguard. Capitalism goes very well with tradition. The systematizing of such a relationship can be called "fascism," to use an old word. Historical fascism or Nazism always remained internal to capitalism and fought fiercely against any alternative model. But, on the other side of the triangle, capitalism is also intrinsically linked to modernity, which secretly corrupts tradition. This is Marx's famous dictum to the effect that capitalism dissolves all stability, all age-old customs, in the "icy waters of egotistical calculation." That dissolving capacity goes hand in hand with the aspects we mentioned: the unlimited promotion of individual freedoms, the dynamic of interests, the exclusive, structuring appearance of the subject before the market, and so on. This breakthrough toward modernity, of which individualism provides the general framework, can easily be inscribed in traditional channels. In previously indifferent or resistant enclaves, capitalism was able to create what I call the "desire for the West," that is, the aspiration to participate in modernity. This desire for the West is an insidious desire for capitalism itself, since you can't obtain the effects without having the cause. This is why the current triumph of capitalism is to a large extent one of the aspects of the victory of modernity over tradition, even if it has that power of attraction and combination of both poles.

Can communism, like capitalism, be connected to the two opposite poles of tradition and modernity?

A.B.: That's clearly the key problem. If we take my diagram and switch to its other side, the side of communism, we encounter the figure of historical communism embodied by the former socialist states. Where they're concerned, communism was unequivocally connected to the pole of tradition. They were ultimately very conservative regimes, in every sphere, at least from the 1930s on: Party control over daily collective life; marriage between comrades; strict family morality; banning of all deviances, including sexual ones; manifest hostility to any kind of esthetic innovation, etc. And to cap it all off, a propaganda whose populist and nationalist character became increasingly blatant. In the late socialist states, all the traditional values to which the people

were attached were maintained, with the notable exception of religion – in that respect, I grant you, we have
indeed had secular religions! But as a result, historical
communism relinquished modernity to capitalism. And
that may be the real reason for its failure. It's often said
that the socialist states failed economically. If you take a
closer look at it, though, that's not so true. In the 1970s,
a little country like the GDR ranked seventh among the
world powers, and the USSR was objectively the only
colossus comparable to the US. Yes, there was plenty
of waste and mismanagement; yes, local supply short-
ages were reported, but the failure was not essentially a
material one. The failure of historical communism was
first and foremost a failure of modernity, of the desire
for modernity, and therefore a subjective failure far
more than an objective one.

**So your idea would be to shift modernity over to com-
munism, to reinvent a communism that would not be
hostile to what is most modern about our times?**

A.B.: I think humanity's destiny – let's have a drumroll
here (*laughter*) – is the possibility for it to invent a non-
capitalist modernity in the present circumstances. In my
diagram, one side of the square remains open: the side
where the conjunction of communism and modernity
occurs. The socialist states weren't able to experiment
with it. They abandoned the terrain of modernity. If
communism is so often ridiculed as an archaic, dreary,
obsolete alternative, it's because its historical realization remained trapped in the straitjacket of tradition.
We need to extricate it from that. Being trapped in it is
not a destiny. This is the task I'm trying to contribute to

philosophically: to sketch the fourth side of the square, to think the potential emergence of a communist modernity. A communism finally capable of modernity. This pursuit leads me to say, once again, that we're back in a situation similar to that of the 1840s in Europe. Somehow, we communists are older than you, who take the early years of the twentieth century as a point of comparison.

M.G.: Far be it from me to overlook the 1840s . . .

A.B.: Of course, I'm well aware that you pay attention to them, as you should! I just wanted to point out that we have a very steep hill to climb. In the 1840s Marx's sole focus was on finding the conditions of a modernity that would not be left just to the capitalists and the champions of private initiative. His task was to lead the way toward true democracy, to move toward its ultimate reality, via the communist project. That challenge is ours today. But you, Marcel Gauchet, don't seem to believe that communism can be merged with modernity . . .

M.G.: The pursuit of a new way of connecting communism and modernity is perfectly legitimate. I will certainly not claim that communism is incapable of modernity. In that respect, we agree: the socialist states did not exhaust the possibilities of the communist idea. They represented a unique historical situation, and we shouldn't draw universal scientific – to use the old Marxist-Leninist lingo – conclusions from their failure. We haven't experienced what communism's ultimate truth might be. The resounding proclamations about the end of history should always arouse suspicion. That has simply not happened. Nor are our societies today the end of the line for humanity.

A.B.: So we agree on rejecting Francis Fukuyama's thesis about the end of history. A common enemy – that's a start!

M.G.: Let's not kick someone when they're down. Fukuyama is too easy a target . . . And, in a way, you're adopting a similar position, insofar as you think there's nothing to hope for from the parliamentary democracies. If that's not another version of the end of history, I don't know what is . . . To come back to what you were saying about the contemporary conflict between tradition and modernity, I think that one of the features of today's European societies is what could be called their "de-traditionalization." The European democracies' palpable disorientation, which is evident in their marginalization throughout the world, is closely linked to this subterranean phenomenon. The conservative or even reactionary upsurges we see today should themselves be interpreted as a kind of fearful reaction to the ineluctable process of de-traditionalization. Here or there, people want to hold on to certain legacies of the past, certain cultural or moral throwbacks. France recently witnessed a campaign of that sort, concerning the family. I don't need to say any more about it. But these convulsions only serve to conceal from those involved the fact that their cause is lost. They're just going to have to deal with it.

For a long time, tradition served as a hidden but very effective scaffolding for our political societies' usual ways of functioning. They were based, for example, on a rather diffuse patriotism, on the power of local leaders, on the social reproduction of representatives elected by universal suffrage. All these traditional elements have gradually faded away, evaporated. The usual codes have changed. That's also why I persist in speaking about a genuine crisis of democracy. The ground under its feet has given way; it has ended up in a vacuum. This is just an observation I've made, but I, for one, am not about to shed any tears over tradition's dead body – other people are doing so. The fact remains that this de-traditionalization presents us with a challenge that is as crucial as it is unprecedented: the democracies have to invent new political mechanisms that are no longer linked to tradition. Either the renewal will occur at a deep level, in every dimension – and, economically, private property as commonly conceived of is the traditional basis of capitalism – or it will not occur at all.

Chapter 8
Why we're not finished with politics

You began this dialogue with a mutual presentation of your intellectual and militant trajectories, from which it emerged that the idea of the subject, whether individual or collective, was the lifeblood of your thinking. Even though it had been brushed aside as an outdated notion by your contemporaries, both of you, in different but consistent ways, have retained the concept of the subject. As we reach the end of this discussion, could we come back to that critical issue? In order for politics to regain a coherent meaning and purpose, in what way should it be linked to individuals' ability to become authentic subjects? In short, what is a political subject? And how is it a key for re-establishing politics, a category that's disparaged today and often reduced to the mere management of everyday affairs?

Alain Badiou: It has in fact become common practice in the diagnoses of the contemporary period to talk about an end of politics and a disappearance of the subject. The notions of "the post-political" and "the post-subjective" are especially fashionable.

Marcel Gauchet: Yes, the prefix "post" is used for anything and everything today. We're supposedly in the age of the post-everything, and I'd add the trendy idea of a "post-democracy" to that list . . .

A.B.: I take issue with that view of things. I've been fighting it right from the start. Both on the purely philosophical level and in the dimension of practice, I try to retain these two categories of politics and subject. More than that, there's a close connection between them, in my view. I note that certain intellectuals who were friends and comrades of mine for a long time – I'm thinking in particular of Sylvain Lazarus – always balked at the notion of the subject, without my regarding that as anything but a purely philosophical difference between us. Ultimately, though, they came to reject the very concept of "politics" and began saying fashionable things about the "end of politics," things that philosophers in the Heideggerian tradition, like some other friends of mine, Philippe Lacoue-Labarthe and Jean-Luc Nancy, were saying by the 1980s. But that tradition had always regarded the notion of "the subject" as metaphysical and obsolete. Yes, at the strictly philosophical level, the concepts of the subject and politics are closely linked. If you deny the relevance of one, you end up denying the relevance of the other. So I had to reconstruct the value of both of them simultaneously.

Before getting to that, though, it may be helpful, as a preliminary, to briefly define what I mean by "the subject." I make a strong distinction between this notion and that of "the individual." In my thinking, a subject is someone who decides to be faithful to an event that rips apart the fabric of his/her purely individualistic and lackluster existence. The event is always unpredictable. It splits open and overturns the stagnant order of the world by opening up new possibilities of life, thought, and action. A political revolution, an amorous encounter, an artistic innovation, a significant scientific discovery are all events. They cause something profoundly new to emerge, they give rise to a hitherto unknown truth – every truth is necessarily linked, and subsequent to, the occurrence of the event. The subject does not remain passive in the face of the event: s/he makes it his/her own and commits firmly to the experience opened up to him/her. The subject denotes that capacity for becoming involved in an event and that willingness to incorporate oneself into a truth, in a lasting process that gives life its true direction. I think there are four main areas in which truths are revealed: politics, love, art, and science. Politics is therefore one of the places where a subject can come into being.

What is specific about it? What is the nature of the intimate connection between the subject and politics, which you mentioned a moment ago?

A.B.: Politics is the dimension of life in which subjects can create a relationship that's universalizable to others and can be born to themselves in that relationship. It's the sphere in which subjects engage in a process that opens them up to themselves, but also opens up the community to which they belong to a universal. We leave behind the realm of solipsistic introspection, of self-absorption. We're no longer limited to abstract thought, the model of which is the natural sciences. Politics makes us, scattered individuals at first, into subjects that embark upon a collective project capable of guiding the common vision of united wills.

In terms of both politics and the subject, my view is totally different from the one prevailing today. What are we told about the subject? That it coincides with its immediate interests, whether economic or personal. To take that line is to dissolve the notion of the subject in the false obviousness of the individual, while genuine politics is dissolved in the "icy waters" of capitalism. Some contemporary American thinkers push this logic quite far. They engage in an almost ontological radicalization of liberalism itself: to explain everything, not just how economies function, they say, you have to work on the assumption that there are individual atoms controlled by their own exclusive interests. To oppose this doctrine, which is intolerable in every respect, the very theory of the subject needs to be changed: the subject will then denote the tendency, the ability to see the community's destiny in terms of its own interest, but not *exclusively* so. It is this "not exclusively so" that, in my opinion, is the focal or nodal point of politics. It is this "not exclusively so" that is the sign of that dimension of universalizability, of a truth's exception, which uproots and overthrows the regime of pure individualism.

Is it from that point of view that the following passage from your book *The Century* should be understood: "If you think that the world can and must change absolutely; that there is neither a nature of things to be respected nor pre-formed subjects to be maintained, you

thereby admit that the individual may be sacrificable"[4]?
Those lines shocked . . .

A.B.: Of course they did! People rushed right into the
trap of misinterpretation. They turned those lines into
a justification of terror, and I was made out to be a
bloodthirsty totalitarian, with a knife between his teeth.
Anyone who knows me can only laugh at such a caricature! It was later supplemented by an accusation that
was even more false, if possible, and above all absolutely
intolerable, not funny in the least, to wit, that I was an
anti-Semite, because I was a universalist! Clearly, there's
no limit to aggressiveness, especially when it links philosophy and politics.

But the truth is, I'm a thoughtful, peace-loving man.
I'm not saying that enemies, even if there are always
some, should be physically exterminated or that supporters should be thrown to the wolves, even if every
real commitment potentially involves risking one's very
life. What I'm saying is that in politics it's very often a
matter of sacrificing the individual in oneself, the strictly
individual figure of one's self, in order to become a
subject. In politics you might come to believe that the
strong convictions you are defending are ultimately
more important than your own little life. That's what
accounts for its – sometimes tragic – grandeur. But it's
always a matter of a fundamental selflessness in political subjectivation. The subject is someone who breaks
free from self-centered demands and obeys transindividual imperatives. This can take the form of a desire

---

[4] Alain Badiou, *The Century*, tr. Alberto Toscano (Cambridge: Polity, 2007), 99.

for equality, an emancipatory aspiration that mobilizes a "we." So let's not leave the subject to the economists, who encapsulate it in the figure of the individual, his/her personal appetites, and his/her petty freedoms.

Marcel Gauchet, does the idea of the subject as an agency capable of binding to an event and a universal truth seem useful to you?

M.G.: The concept of the subject, which is also central to my own project, is formidably difficult. It's impossible to gloss over its complexity. But we still have to try to speak simply about it. To understand the issues involved, we need to start by freeing it from its ordinary meaning, a meaning that has become the dominant one in current philosophical language. The subject is subjectivity, that is, interiority. In short, the subject is me. From this perspective, the notion is of no interest. Then there's a second meaning, which is historical, in line with what philosophy since German idealism has tried to define as a specificity of the modern age. The subject is the name of certain experiences or states of humanity that have been made possible by modernity.

To get a clearer picture, a distinction should be made between the individual, the person, and the subject. Humanity, like the other animal species, is made up of individuals in the biological sense of the term. A distinctive feature of these biological individuals is that they are endowed with presence to self and self-reflexivity: they have a sense of their own identity in the context of communities that are also self-identified. This is what makes them persons who recognize each other as such. But, in addition, over the course of modernity and thanks to what I have called the exit from religion, these persons have changed from within and become subjects. Once humanity no longer sees itself in terms of an Other who gives it the key to its identity but relates to itself under the principle of autonomy, it enters the age of subjectivity. The exit from religion comes down to eliminating otherness from the definition of self, finding one's own justification in oneself. Whereas humanity was once subject to something higher than itself, it has now become the subject of itself. But we still need to specify how this transformation of the idea and practice of self came about.

The terrain of modern science and the new form it has given to the knowledge process has been the privileged, matricial site of this experience. This is what philosophy since Descartes has been attempting to think as the subject of science, or the subject of reason, capable of universal knowledge. But modernity's distinguishing feature is to broaden this dimension of the subject to include other registers of human experience: ethics, esthetics, or politics. In each of these areas "the subject" and "subjectivity" denote not a permanent property of the actor, a continuous state that would define him/her in general, but a stage which s/he reaches in specific situations. A scientist can become a "subject" when performing his/her job as a scientist and cease to be one when s/he takes off his/her lab coat and spouts nonsense in the local café. What is the demarcation criterion? It is the goal of obtaining a universally valid result that will give shape to his/her scientific practice, while in the local café his/her opinions are nobody's business but his/her own. Due to the rigorousness of the concept, "subject" applies not to a constitutive attribute of what we are but to an experience that people can have under certain conditions. It is a completely original, historically arrived-at feature or quality of human existence. We are subjects at well-defined moments, and we are so when a universal is involved in our action. Politics is one of the possible modes of subjectivation. It's not the only one. But it's a major one, and we should remember this, because the properly political dimension of the history of modern subjectivity is too often forgotten. Yet the issue of the subject lies behind the founding reflections of modern political philosophy, from Hobbes to Rousseau. Since then, for various reasons, it has been somewhat lost sight of.

What is your analysis of the constitution of the political subject?

M.G.: I believe we need to speak about a double subjectivation. Politics is the sphere of human experience in which an individual and a collective subjectivation are connected. An individual's becoming a subject involves self-abandonment, which makes it possible to take on the constitutive rules of the social contract or of the formation of a general will. The political subject comes to itself by becoming actively involved in this process. But there's also a collective subject that emerges from the fusion of the individual wills. The collective subject is not a hypostasis separate from its components. It can be challenged or eliminated by the very persons who formed it, in accordance with mechanisms agreed on beforehand. But its figure is what ultimately gives meaning to the idea of self-government. Political subjectivation, politics *tout court*, in the democratic framework, is nothing other than this dynamic connecting the individual and the collective, in which the two spheres interact with and interpenetrate each other.

A.B.: I completely agree with you.

M.G.: For once – that's great!

A.B.: I agree about both the general philosophical conception of the subject and your approach to politics. The idea of a double subjectivation seems quite right to me. It clearly has both theoretical and descriptive relevance. But let's not end our *disputatio* on a partly artificial agreement . . . We agree on the need to restore the conditions of a properly political subjectivation. But, in my view, the ability to become a political subject requires a very serious withdrawal from the already existing collective constraint. The current dominant imperatives, however, are dictated and corrupted enormously by the hegemony of economics. Therefore, achieving the subjective possibility of politics and reviving politics itself involve an unconditional detachment, a radical separation, from the system of constraints and obligations imposed by the capitalist complex. Re-politicizing and re-subjectivating require the formulation and testing of the communist hypothesis as the only conceivable and viable alternative to the financial oligarchy's overwhelming power.

With the collapse of the socialist countries, we actually entered an era of profound depoliticization and desubjectivation. As the despotic socialist states once did, capitalism, free of any alternative to it, is wiping out politics and slowly strangling the subject. The communist hypothesis frees us from that deadly grip by offering new support for a way out. It's just as with Plato's cave: the slave who escapes and discovers the real world, uncontaminated by the sham of appearances. Except that the world that the communist hypothesis claims is possible isn't a purely intelligible world; it's a real world, which can and must come into being in *our* world. We'll never achieve this, we'll never revive a genuine, intense, creative, and emancipatory politics, if we trust the parliamentary democracies, precisely because they are themselves prisoners of the worldwide capitalist cave . . .

M.G.: Let me go back and insist on the logic of the connection between the individual and the collective. It's at the heart of the democratic experience itself. Democracy isn't synonymous with desubjectivation . . .

A.B.: I didn't say that.

M.G.: Yes, but once again, you make it sound as though the liberal democracies are forever condemned to powerlessness in the face of the dominance of economics.

A.B.: That is in fact what I believe. That's my position. In terms of regaining control, parliamentary democracy is finished. Clearly, we'll never agree . . .

M.G.: In what sense can democracy be the very experience of the double subjectivation whose model I sketched? There's a writer who already answered this question perfectly: Rousseau. It was he who, as the introducer of the individualist scheme into European thought, conceived of the world that's become our

world and gave democracy its very meaning. Before
being an institutional setup, democracy is the experience or the time of a basic agreement: the agreement of
an individual who constitutes him/herself as a citizen
with the community to which s/he belongs. Without
feeling as though s/he is giving up his/her natural freedom at all, the citizen identifies with a collective cause
that transcends him/her and in whose immanence s/he
grounds him/herself. This collective cause was freely
and deliberately defined: by taking part in the choice,
in the decision, the individual binds him/herself to the
collective, bypassing the private sphere of his/her own
interests – this is Rousseau's famous, fundamental distinction between the general will and the will of all (as
a simple addition of individual wills). At the very heart
of the democratic experience there is this conjunction of
the individual and the collective, which ultimately leads
to the formulation of the universal object that a political community can set itself. This universal object, with
which the subjects are in relation, is usually linked to
justice. The democratic idea lies in this ability to guide
the double – individual and collective – subjectivation
toward the universal, using the modern political means
of autonomy. What separates us from Rousseau is precisely the means that have been used over the past two
centuries. They have made us lose sight of the regulating
ideal which can alone give meaning to their use.

For if this constitutive dimension is overlooked, then,
indeed, all we will see in democracy is an empty shell, a
political form replicating the economic market: citizens
are consumers, they go to vote in elections the way they
go to the supermarket to choose the best product, and
so on. This is the sorry spectacle presented by the con-

temporary situation. We agree about this assessment. The true meaning of democracy has been lost as a result of the changes I noted earlier – which can be summed up as the demise of collective power for the benefit of the primacy of individual rights. Today's liberal democracies are so far removed from the Rousseauian ideal that we might conclude it's no longer the least bit relevant. But such is not actually the case. It is still at work subterraneously, and I believe this in many respects explains the feelings of frustration, dispossession, and revolt harbored by many of our fellow citizens. So we should definitely not think that the current crisis has the final word on the issue. We have the means to get out of it by going back to the very source of the democratic idea and adapting that idea to what Rousseau couldn't have imagined, i.e., the concrete organization of an autonomous world.

A.B.: The Rousseau reference doesn't bother me at all. He's a key philosopher for me too. But when you refer to justice as the norm of democracy, what are you talking about exactly? The fact that the citizens assemble and choose their rulers by themselves cannot ensure the effectiveness of justice. The mechanisms peculiar to parliamentary democracy can turn out to be completely ineffectual or even counterproductive to the attainment of the ideal you hold so dear. No, essentially, justice involves the extreme protest against the big Other. If justice can and is to be achieved, it requires attacking capital head on. The truth is, if democracy is defined by the Idea of justice, then the real democratic subject is a communist subject! But by your own admission, the democratic subject is blocked, caught in the chains of contemporary capitalism. How can you expect to free the subject by preserving the politico-institutional apparatus that is irremediably subjected to capitalism? I'm very pessimistic about your hypothesis ... In principle, I have no objection to continuing the democratic enterprise as you've defined it. Along that path, moreover, you'll encounter communism as an inevitable principle, the only one that can finally make egalitarian democracy a reality. But in practice, I don't see how that would be possible. I fear that your reformist perspective is tragically inadequate for political subjectivation to be re-established to its full extent and that in the final analysis it's only committed to hopeless quick fixes.

M.G.: I think, on the contrary, that the range of reformist opportunities is extremely wide. And there's a danger inherent in the communist hypothesis in that it has a tendency to give precedence to one kind of subjectivation over the other: individual subjectivity absorbed back into and swallowed up in collective subjectivity. The Whole absorbing its parts ...

A.B.: Careful! That's not at all *my* communist hypothesis you're describing. It's precisely your own fusional, unary conception of totalitarian societies. Please, don't surreptitiously inject totalitarianism into my thinking – it already has a bad enough reputation as it is! I have never argued that everyone should become a subject all at once, at the same time. That's what Robespierre, for his part, wanted, and those who weren't sufficiently subjects in his eyes became suspect for just that reason ... When an event makes new figures of subjectivation possible, it never encompasses *all* individuals: to determine who will become a subject, you have to monitor what's really going on, the participation in assemblies and deliberations, different people's fidelity to the inaugural event. Whatever the case may be, I remain convinced that if there is to be a political event, it will have to break with the general logic of the contemporary world.

Conclusion:
In search of a lost deal?

Alain Badiou: Marcel Gauchet, I'd like to conclude by sharing the insight I had when I was listening to you speak about Rousseau and the possibility of a collective political subject that goes by the name of democracy. I think it's fair to say that I'm actually not the only one waiting for an event . . .

Marcel Gauchet: How so? What do you mean?

A.B.: I think that, in spite of your cautiousness, you believe in politics and, for that reason, you're waiting for an event in the sense I've given that term. An event that's unforeseeable, like every event, but which makes it possible to bring about a new reformist subjectivity . . .

M.G.: Maybe . . .

A.B.: In order for this event to emerge, I'd like to make you acknowledge that you have a fundamental need for the communist hypothesis. Let me explain this point, which is at once historical, tactical, and philosophical, to you. You seem to think that the communist hypothesis is of no use to you for carrying out your ambitious reformism. I'd answer that that's not at all the case. In recent history, the rare periods that more or less approximate what you have in mind were only achieved because of the actual presence of the other world, the other hypothesis – the communists. The major reformist resurgence that occurred after 1945, to which you often referred, was only possible because De Gaulle had to come to an understanding with the French Communist Party, which was the most powerful party in France back then, basking in its reputation as "the Party of the 100,000 executed." At the Liberation, the General had international allies, to be sure, credibility with the military authorities, but a majority of the civilian troops, so to speak, were on the other side . . . I don't think that De Gaulle was a mortal enemy of capitalism at heart, or a strong supporter of nationalizations. But he had to bargain and make concessions . . . Nowadays, the National Council of the Liberation's program is held up as an example of the return to democracy. But that Council stated that De Gaulle was obligated to come to an understanding with the Communists! The deal between them should not be considered as a deal inherent in the general evolution of capitalism but as a deal dictated by the circumstances of the existence of the communist parties and the Soviet bloc. And the context of the reconstruction, with its own economic and political imperatives, explains why the capitalist predators behaved nicely and complied with the significant reforms that went against their interests. This broad consensus later crumbled as the Communist bloc broke apart. Ever since historical communism collapsed for good, the democracies have no longer been challenged by their communist enemy. The neoliberal wave you oppose swept in and filled the vacuum. In the absence of an Other threatening them, the liberal democracies have once again become the vassals of capital and its owners, who no longer feel compelled to accept the principles of moderation and redistribution.

M.G.: As far as the 1945 period is concerned, that's historically accurate.

A.B.: But that historical moment also had tactical and philosophical implications for the present time. Unless the communist hypothesis is revived, the reformist hypothesis you defend has no chance of becoming a reality. Apart from strategy, it may also mean that democracy itself needs to be shaped by otherness, whether internal or external to its form. So, in the end, it's you who ought to thank *me*! You won't get anywhere, practically speaking, without me. I'm actually offering to help you out!

M.G.: Yes, please, scare the hell out of them in order to give us a big helping hand! As for me, I'm sticking with liberal democracy, and true change is more within my reach than within yours, if I may put it that way. But I can't resist the temptation to answer you: by offering to help me out, you're implicitly acknowledging that the communist hypothesis you're reviving is weak on its own and will only have "reality effects" in the compromises that it will make possible to reach within the reformed democracies. You want to make me say that consistent reformism needs to be backed by the communist hypothesis? I readily admit that we need all the help we can get to achieve political control of neoliberal globalization. I'd even add that the communist hypothesis, which I would personally prefer to call "the communist utopia," like the anarchist utopia, is by necessity inscribed in the horizon of our societies, as a projection of the principle of equal freedom that founds them. I therefore think that we just have to accept it. But on your side, by making the communist hypothesis a necessary ally of democratic realism you're clipping the wings of your radicalism. That's an honest admission! And it will allow us to seal the deal you're proposing.

A.B.: A grand alliance at the end of such a contentious debate? Our deal will never eliminate our differences, and I will never be on the side of parliamentary democracy, but sure, why not? This is an unexpected outcome, to say the least! Even the bitterest opponents can agree if they're able to acknowledge that, in the end, they're each, individually and using their own weapons, fighting the same enemy.

Appendix

Alain Badiou's diagram of the contemporary structure of the world

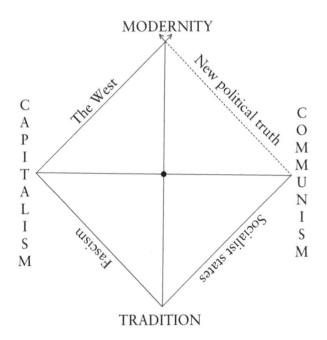

Index

Index

Index

Index